ISBN: 978-0-9830768-3-4

Library of Congress Control Number: 2011923809

Published by Exit Zero Publishing, Inc.,
109 Sunset Boulevard, Suite D,
Cape May, NJ 08204
www.exitzero.us/publishing
IN CONJUNCTION WITH ANNE LEDUC

Cover postcard courtesy of Will Valentine
Postcard on previous page courtesy of Don Pocher

Book edited and designed by
Jack Wright

Contents

Foreword ....Page 5

Chapter I   **Hotel For A Hero**...Page 6

Chapter II   **Southern Belle Goes North** ....Page 22

Chapter III   **Satterfields Are Here To Stay**......................Page 42

Chapter IV   **Keeping Her In The Family**............................Page 66

Chapter V   **Saved By The Architects** ....Page 88

Chapter VI   **Weekend Warriors**.......................................Page 112

Chapter VII   **Perennial Guests: Naughty And Nice** ....Page 128

Chapter VIII   **The Soul Of The Chalfonte**.........................Page 164

Chapter IX   **Rogues, Entrepreneurs And Adventurers** ....Page 186

Chapter X   **Art And Artists At The Chalfonte** ....Page 208

Chapter XI   **A History Of Romance**................................Page 224

Chapter XII   **Old Meets New: The Mullock Mission**.............Page 240

Bibliography...Page 256

Early researchers believed the word Chalfont derived from the old English *chald* (cold) and *funt* (spring). Spoken quickly, the word *chaldfunt* became chalfont, meaning cold springs. Henry Sawyer, who built and named the Chalfonte Hotel, lived in the village of Cold Spring and was married, and buried, at Cold Spring Presbyterian Church.

Foreword

I HAVE been wanting to write a book about the Chalfonte for years. And for years, everyone has said, "You should write a book!" Recently, I decided it was time, and I commissioned a team to put this book together. Karen Fox did an exceptional job researching and writing the history of the old hotel; she has told the Chalfonte story in a way that makes it come alive for those of us who have lived portions of the hotel's history, and fascinating to those who have not. Jack Wright assembled a layout of photos and text that together paint a beautiful picture of one of America's national treasures – he is a master of creative and tasteful design. It isn't easy to tell the story of this architectural and historic gem, but this book captures the essence of the Chalfonte.

And lastly, none of this would have been possible without my friend and business partner, Judy Bartella, who helped save the hotel and whose input enhanced this book. I hope you enjoy the story of the Chalfonte.

Anne LeDuc, Moorestown, NJ, February, 2011

THE way to Cape May for me was initiated more than 40 years ago by a lovely Virginian by the name of Roberta Kyle Randolph West. Roberta's mother, Catharine Pleasants, of Richmond, vacationed in 1917 at the Chalfonte, where she met her husband, attorney Robert Butterworth of Philadelphia. Roberta lived nearby, in Lansdowne, Pennsylvania and had a summer home at Cape May Point.

Another Lansdowne resident, hockey athlete Courtney Solenberger (McNeill), introduced me to Anne LeDuc, saying, "If you're in Cape May you need to spend time with Anne, the maestro of the Chalfonte." I took Courtney's advice.

Four decades and dozens of Cape May summers later, the circle closes with the story of the Chalfonte safely between covers. The pleasure has been all mine, meeting the cast of characters past and present who have made the historic Chalfonte – the leading lady – one of the most magical places on the planet.

This book is dedicated to my husband John Eric Schneider, for his enduring enthusiasm and patience. And to Anne LeDuc for the opportunity.

Karen Fox, Chalfonte Hotel porch, Labor Day, 2010

CHAPTER I
Hotel For A Hero

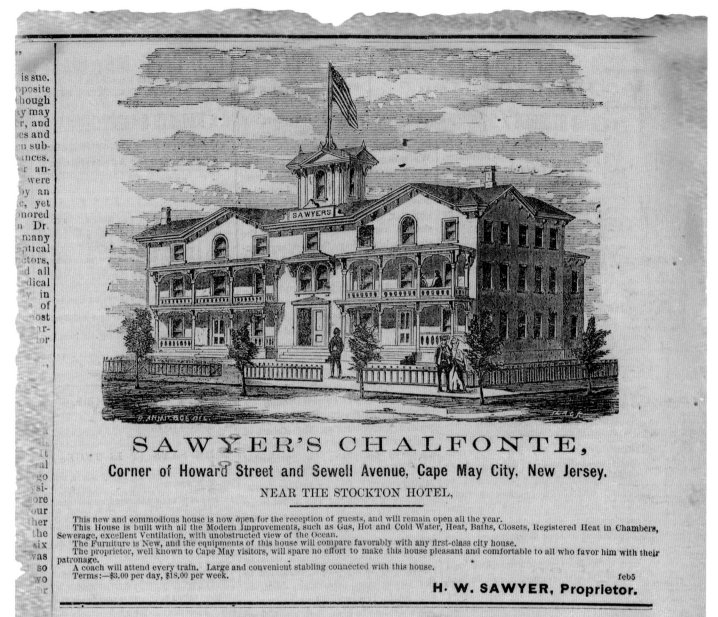

SAWYER'S CHALFONTE,
Corner of Howard Street and Sewell Avenue, Cape May City, New Jersey.
NEAR THE STOCKTON HOTEL,

This new and commodious house is now open for the reception of guests, and will remain open all the year.
    This House is built with all the Modern Improvements, such as Gas, Hot and Cold Water, Heat, Baths, Closets, Registered Heat in Chambers, Sewerage, excellent Ventilation, with unobstructed view of the Ocean.
    The Furniture is New, and the equipments of this house will compare favorably with any first-class city house.
    The proprietor, well known to Cape May visitors, will spare no effort to make this house pleasant and comfortable to all who favor him with their patronage.
    A coach will attend every train. Large and convenient stabling connected with this house.
    Terms:—$3.00 per day, $18.00 per week.

feb5

H. W. SAWYER, Proprietor.

GEORGE W. SMITH.   J. P. HENRY.

CAPE May was emerging from a deep economic depression in 1875, the year the Chalfonte was being built. The post-Civil War building boom bubble burst in 1873. Large banks failed and money was scarce. But Henry Sawyer, a Civil War hero and local developer, was not deterred – there was regular train service from Philadelphia, and Grant Street Summer Station was under construction. Sawyer anticipated his new hotel would be a full house.

The *Cape May Wave* newspaper announced

PROUD PROPRIETOR
Chalfonte builder Henry Sawyer published more ads than any other hotel owner in the local newspaper. This vintage clipping was found by Cape May print shop owner Heidi Cummings.

FACING THE FUTURE
Opposite page: A young Henry Sawyer could not have imagined the adventures that lay before him, taking him on to the nation's bloodiest battlefields.
Donlin collection

in April, 1875 that local builder Charles Shaw would be erecting "a rooming cottage" for Sawyer. By June the cottage was finished. Work continued to erect a twin of the first building and the two were joined, with a central double entry and a cupola on top. The new Chalfonte stood handsome and imposing in its eclectic Victorian style at Howard Street and Sewell Avenue, two blocks from the Atlantic Ocean. Across the street a sprawling lawn set the stage for the favorite Victorian games of cricket and croquet.

Sawyer advertised his new Chalfonte in the *Wave* every week. His ad was the largest in the paper, showing off his new hotel and trumpeting its amenities. The plan was to attract

A Certain Style

The same year the Chalfonte was under construction, wealthy cotton and wool merchant Alexander Whilldin and department store owner John Wanamaker formed the Sea Grove Association, "a moral and religious seaside home" for Presbyterians at Cape May Point. They carved the development from the wilderness based on a design by nationally famous architect James Charles Sidney. Also in 1875, Whilldin built a Victorian cottage (pictured above) on the beach at Sea Grove called Land's End. With its broad verandas, gingerbread and cupola, it looked similar to the Chalfonte.
Photo courtesy of Cape May County Museum and Genealogical Society

vacationers who were traveling to Cape May by express train – the trip from Philadelphia took less than three hours. A return ticket cost $2.50, while a season ticket, from June 1 to October 1, cost $50. Here is how Sawyer's ad read:

SAWYER'S CHALFONTE
Corner of Howard and Sewell Avenues, Cape May, Near the Stockton Hotel.

This new and commodious house will be open January 1st, 1876, for reception of guests and will remain open all year. This house is built with all the modern improvements such as Gas, Hot and Cold Water, Heat, Baths, Closets, Registered Heat in Chambers, sewerage, excellent Ventilation, with unobstructed view of the

ocean. The Furniture is new and the entire equipments of this house will compare favorably with any first class city house. The Proprietor, well known to Cape May visitors, will spare no effort to make this house pleasant and comfortable to all who favor him with their patronage. A coach will attend every train. Large and convenient stabling connected with this house.

Terms – $3.00 per day, $18 per week until June 1st, 1876.

– H. W. Sawyer Proprietor

The Chalfonte opened the same year the nation celebrated its Centennial at Fairmount Park in Philadelphia. The country was still healing from the Civil War but was proud of its burgeoning machine age and railroads that now stretched across much of the nation.

"One hundred years ago our country was new and but partially settled..." said Ulysses Grant, the victorious Civil War general elected president, in opening remarks May 10, 1876, in Philadelphia. American flags with 37 stars fluttered on the Centennial grounds. Exhibits from around the world excited 100,000 visitors that first day. Ten million fairgoers attended the exhibition in 1876 while Henry Sawyer welcomed his first guests to the Chalfonte.

Sawyer himself was an attraction. Less than 10 years earlier, he had been left for dead on a battlefield in Virginia. He was shot in the head, and lay unconscious next to his wounded horse. His cavalry unit moved on, and a Confederate burial squad found Sawyer the next morning. He survived his wounds but was incarcerated at the squalid Libby Prison, only to face death again – this time by firing squad.

Sawyer was born Henry Washington Saeger, a German farm boy, on March 16, 1829, in Egypt, Lehigh County, Pennsylvania. He helped on the family farm, attended Normal School and was a carpentry apprentice. He was devoted to woodworking, but his biggest passion was horses. At 19, he learned of a carpenter's job in Cape May. The year was 1848. His mother and father objected, but Henry negotiated his way away from the farm and traveled a few days and 150 miles from the fertile fields of Egypt to the ocean. Henry settled in Eldredge (now West Cape May) and changed his name from Saeger (Saw Man) to Sawyer. He was described as five foot, 10 1/2 inches, weighing about 190 pounds.

Two years later, in 1850, he married Harriet Eldredge, daughter of a prominent family for which the town Eldredge was named. The wedding was at Cold Spring Presbyterian Church, the old brick church on Seashore Road, which looks today much the way it did 160 years ago. During the first year of his marriage Sawyer built a home, paid it off, and two years later sold it for double the price. The couple had three children, but only their daughter Louisa survived. Tommy died of typhoid fever at age two; and in 1864, the second son, also named Tommy, died aged nine.

Sawyer's early days in Cape May coincided with a building boom as the seashore town grew in size and stature as the nation's first resort. Many summer visitors were from the south, especially Virginia. It was the antebellum era in Washington and Cape May.

Despite Cape May's hospitality to the southern planters, and the financial gain from the relationships, the locals were turning their backs on the strengthening Confederacy. There were considerable anti-southern, anti-slavery sentiments arising in South Jersey. A month

NEGATIVE BY J. GARDNER.

SAWYER'S MEN
Near the end of the war, Colonel Sawyer, third from left in the front row, served at the Cavalry Headquarters at Camp Stoneman, Washington, DC, which accommodated up to 12,000 horses for drilling and training.
Donlin collection

POSITIVE BY A. GARDNER

cidents of the War

after Lincoln took office a Cape May group of pro-slavery men hoisted South Carolina's Palmetto flag at Decatur and Washington Streets. Sawyer, a vociferous opponent of the Confederacy, was among the crowd that pulled down the flag and burned it in the street.

With war concerns top of mind, Sawyer checked the telegraph office regularly. On April 12, 1861, he learned the US garrison at Fort Sumter, South Carolina, had fallen to the Confederacy. Two days later, President Lincoln called for 75,000 volunteers to put down the rebels.

Sawyer was among the first to answer President Lincoln's call. A New Jersey regiment had not been formed so Governor Charles Olden sent Sawyer as a messenger to the Secretary of War in Washington.

Sawyer wrote a battlefield diary, which he titled "Lottery of Death, a Narrative of the War." Here he relays the moves that led to war...

It was my good fortune to arrive in Washington the morning of April 16th, with dispatches from the Governor of New Jersey, Charles S. Olden, to Simon Cameron, Secretary of War – telegraphic and mail communication being unsafe.

I found that the loyal people, Congress, and the

CAVALRY CARNAGE
The Battle of Brandy Station was the largest, bloodiest, and most fiercely fought cavalry conflict ever staged on the North American continent.
Library of Congress

BATTLEFIELD DIARY
Opposite: Henry Sawyer, in his bold hand, with fountain pen, wrote vivid war reports from the bloody battlefield and rat-infested Libby Prison. Sawyer's writing was as straightforward as a news reporter's. In this dispatch, detailing the death of men and horses, he writes that "Nationals and Confederates men here fell as the leaves fall in autumn."
Sawyer family

President were in a high state of excitement, – for it was known to them that Maryland and Virginia troops were to assault the city, depending on the disloyal element within, to fire the different portions of the city, and under this terror and confusion, possession was to be taken by those troops of all the public buildings...

Meetings were held in a little church back of Willard's hotel, and solemn were the addresses of distinguished loyal men. Four hundred of us this night, took the oath of fidelity to our Nation's flag, the Constitution and the Union.

In Washington, Sawyer joined the first Pennsylvania volunteer infantry to arrive in the capital city. On April 18, 1861, Sawyer signed up for three months as a private with the 25th Pennsylvania Volunteer Infantry that stood guard at barricades protecting the Capitol.

Sawyer wrote:

Four hundred men composing Reading's Ringgold Battery of Artillery – Captain McKnight – fully mounted and equipped, two companies of Infantry from Pottsville and one company from Allentown, Pennsylvania – all drilled, armed and equipped – and three hundred regular cavalry from the command of General Twiggs...

The arrival of these troops created great excitement,

but its horses mostly killed and
around this battery were lying
both men and horses

Nationa and confederates
men here fell as the leaves
fall in Autumn
— The guns we left —
Now our work was done and
down the hill our troops now go
reforming our broken ranks

Brave as were our troops on our
side
Those on the other fought with
equal desperation

But now behold the Rebel Brigades
of LEE. Hampton & Jones on
our left advancing

There is one incident occurred, that I must mention.

Our troops had passed up the main street in pursuit of the enemy and his train, and on their return, discovered what few of us had ever seen – a slave pen. By natural instinct, not by command, the column halted. An old pile of lumber was lying on the street. The men secured a heavy piece of timber, and without orders or confusion, rammed open the high iron gates and next the iron doors of the building were staved in.

Here were collected all the negroes of Alexandria and its vicinity – free or slave – regardless of condition, age or sex. The building was crowded on every floor. It was intended to move them further south, but our surprise party had prevented it.

The negroes were terribly frightened, old and young, men and women and children, mothers with babes in their arms, were all screaming in terror, having been told that the Yankees would sell them all to Cuba to pay for the expenses of the war.

This was the first slave pen opened by the war, not through any order or command, but purely by the impulse of our better nature. Our officers, however, received a reprimand.

Sawyer was discharged as a sergeant from the Pennsylvania volunteer unit on July 23, 1861.

Events moved very swiftly these early days of the war. After spending less than a month at home in Cape May, Sawyer enlisted again, on August 14, 1861, this time with the First Regiment Cavalry, the New Jersey Volunteers. The unit first gathered on their horses in Washington and then moved out into the fields of war on Virginia's beautiful summer landscape.

Sawyer and his cavalrymen were one of the most aggressive units of the war, fighting in 97 battles. Sawyer, then a captain, was seriously injured in 1862 at Woodstock, Virginia. His horse was shot from under him, stumbled and fell on Sawyer's right leg. The leg healed, but Sawyer was left in pain and endured a limp for the remainder of his life.

There was more to come. Sawyer was leading a small group on a reconnaissance mission near Aldie, Virginia on Halloween, 1862. The thunder of hoofs startled the spy team. Suddenly, 1,500 fast-riding Confederate cavalrymen were upon them. Sawyer lingered behind to give cover for his men to escape. There was gunfire all around and a bullet ripped into Sawyer's stomach, lodging near his spine. Military surgeons were afraid to operate in fear of paralyzing him for life and Sawyer was sent home to recover. Civilian surgeons removed the bullet

as they took up their line of March through Washington escorted by a company of the Clay battalion, of which I was one. Whilst wending their way to the White House to pay respect to our Nation's Chief, swearing could be heard on every side from the rebels.

Mr. Lincoln welcomed them in the most impassioned language, closing the remarks with suppressed emotion, and tears in his eyes, he fervently said: 'God bless you boys.'

On April 19, 1861, Sawyer wrote:

The North was now fully aroused.

From the green hills of Vermont and the dense forests of Maine, from the mills and manufactures of Massachusetts, New York and Pennsylvania, from New Jersey's pines and her sea-shore, from the mighty West, from every section of our country, came brave, determined and patriotic men to protect the honor of our flag and nation...

The first aggressive move of this army was the taking of Alexandria, Virginia, May 14th, 1861...

FAMILY MAN
Henry Sawyer and wife Harriet, who lived out the war years with their three children at their home in Eldredge, now West Cape May. Sawyer wrote to his wife from the battlefield and prison. His passionate plea to his wife prompted her to appeal to President Lincoln personally to free her husband from execution. Her swift action is credited with saving her husband's life.
Donlin collection

without consequence.

But the greatest battle, the most serious wounds, and a terrible ordeal were yet to come.

June 9, 1863, The Battle of Brandy Station, Virginia: Imagine 20,000 men on horseback, armed with sabers and muskets, moving their horses into position. This was the largest, bloodiest, and most fiercely fought cavalry battle ever on the North American continent.

The First New Jersey Cavalry was in the advance, and in Sawyer's handwritten account:

It was now evident that the action was about to begin, and all were eager and enthusiastic. Cheer after cheer was given for our regiment by the other troops, as we passed through their ranks, invigorating every man and inspiring our very horses with the excitement... I was senior Captain and placed me at the head of the regiment. By my side rode Major Shellmire, whilst Lieut. Col. Broderick was on the extreme left.

The command to draw saber and form squadrons was given... 'Use nothing but the cold steal' shouts Sir Percy Wyndham... The bugle now sounds the charge. Steady, steady there, close up, are the words of com-

FAMILY TREASURE
Prominent Philadelphia attorney, the late Henry W. Sawyer III, with his grandfather's Civil War saber. Right: Henry III at age 10, showing off the family heirloom at his grandmother Mary McKissick Sawyer's home on Benton Avenue in Cape May. He inherited the sword when she passed away. It is now owned by the Civil War hero's great-grandson, Hal.

Donlin collection

mand – the officers watching intently their squadrons. Every horse is now doing his best. Their battery now opens with shot and shell, but with too much elevation.

Forward! Onward, we press regardless of the battery's fire. We reach the hill. A terrible hand to hand encounter now ensues. The Confederate cavalry use their pistols – their cannoneers, their sponge staffs, for defense. Our troops, nothing but the saber and the weight of horse in their attack. But now fresh troops arrive upon the field, and with superior force and desperate effort, the Confederates recharge and regain their battery.

Nationals and Confederates men here fell as the leaves fall in autumn. Our troops gave back volley for volley, shott for shott, almost death for death.

The Pennsylvanians now come to our assistance and with Kilpatrick's NY 2nd and Maine's regiment to our support again we charge and retake the guns. In this charge I fell wounded, unconscious and helpless.

Lying close by me, in the last agonies of death was our sturdy Major Shellmire... and not far distant, lay dead our impetuous, noble and brave Lieut. Col. Broderick. Sir Percy, our valiant Colonel, was here wounded.

Two bullets pierced Sawyer's body. One passed through his thigh. The second struck his right check and passed out the back of his neck. Sawyer had remained in the saddle until his horse was shot from under him. His horse reared in the air, then fell dead, tossing Sawyer to the ground, unconscious.

Carnage surrounded Sawyer. There were hundreds of dead and wounded. Devoted horses, having suffered wounds, moaned in pain. Other horses had lost their riders and galloped away in fear. Sawyer lay still as darkness enveloped him and the hours passed.

In his battlefield diary Sawyer wrote:

A terrible night I spent. Water, water, oh for water were the request of the dying without avail.

During the night a wounded Confederate gave me the last drop of water in his canteen to moisten my fevered lips.

A Confederate burial team found Sawyer among the dead. They carted him to a nearby house at Culpepper where, hours later, he was treated for his wounds. There was doubt that Sawyer would live.

During the battle at Brandy Station, a Confederate cavalryman was seriously wounded. His name – General William Henry Fitzhugh

LIFE AND DEATH DRAMA
Robert E. Lee's son, William Henry Fitzhugh Lee "Roonie," left, was taken prisoner and exchanged for Henry Sawyer, who was facing a firing squad. Sawyer's Libby Prison cellmate John M. Flinn, right, was a Catholic, and a bishop was successful in delaying Flinn and Sawyer's execution, giving Flinn time to prepare for death.
Donlin collection

PRISON PAPERS
Opposite: Dated July 4, 1863, the order for execution of two Union soldiers chosen by lottery. Sawyer was selected.
Donlin collection

"Roonie" Lee, the son of General Robert E. Lee, Commander of the Confederate forces. These two men, locked in battle, both seriously wounded, both taken prisoner, would be players in a political tug-of-war for the next two years.

Sawyer was transported to Libby Prison in Richmond, infamous for its poor treatment of captured Union soldiers. Lee, suffering a saber cut and a gunshot wound that narrowly missed a main artery, was rescued from the battlefield by friends and taken by ambulance to his father-in-law General Wickham's plantation, in Hanover County, 18 miles from Richmond. His recovery was cut short by a Union raiding party of 1,000 cavalrymen – he was taken prisoner and locked up at the Union's Fortress Monroe.

July 6, 1863 was a searingly hot day at Libby Prison. Confederate officer Captain Turner strode in and ordered that all imprisoned captains be brought from their quarters to a lower room. Captain Sawyer and his cellmate, Captain John Flinn of Indiana, were excited to be moved after a month in the hot, dank cell. They anticipated an exchange or parole, and perhaps a trip home. Quite the contrary. Captain Turner announced that two captains would be selected by lottery to be executed in retaliation for the

MEMORANDUM FROM PRISONER OF WAR RECORDS.

(This blank to be used only in the arrangement of said records.)

No. _____

| NAME. | RANK. | ORGANIZATION. | | | | INFORMATION OBTAINED FROM— | | | |
		No. of Reg't.	State.	Arm of Service.	Co.	Records of—	Vol.	Page.	Vol.
H. W.						M. Roll	970 —		
awyer, Henry W.	Capt	1	N. J.	C		Mis.	106½.79		

Captured at _____, 186 , confined at Richmond, Va., _____, 18

in accordance with order from Genl. Winder, dated Richmond, Va., July 4.63, to see

Admitted to Hospital at by lot from among the Federal Captains now in his cust

where he died two of that number, 186 , for execution; Capt. Turner Comr

C.S. Mil. Prison, reports July 7th 1863; reported at Camp Parole, Md., that Captain

Sawyer is one of those selected X Federal prisoner in confinement at Richd. Va., July

ving been selected by lot to be executed as a measure of retaliation, protests against said execution.

Copied by C.C.R.

Let this remain —

---

shooting deaths of two Confederate officers who were accused of being spies.

The officers stood in a square and each wrote his name on a slip of paper and placed it in a box. Captain Sawyer was the first to break the silence and suggested that chaplains draw the names. With hesitation, Reverend Joseph Brown agreed. From Sawyer's notes:

Silently consenting, amid death-like stillness, he reverentially drew the first name – it was my own; the second, John M. Flinn of Indiana...

To Camp Lee is the order – our destination being the place for all military executions... Now on the march, we accidentally encountered the carriage of Bishop Lynch of Charlestown, South Carolina, who seeing the two priests with us [Flinn was Roman Catholic] stopped and asked its meaning, the facts being quickly told...

We resumed our march to Camp Lee and were nearing... when an officer well mounted and riding at desperate speed, overtook us... Through the interposition of Bishop Lynch a 10 days respite had been granted, that Capt. Flinn might have time to prepare himself for absolution... I asked of Genl. Winder to be permitted to write a letter to my wife, which was granted. This letter was written under a severe strain of nerve.

Sawyer wrote the following letter to his wife Harriet:

Libby Prison
Richmond, Virginia
July 6th, 1863

From The Archives

Excerpt from *The Richmond Dispatch* newspaper, dated July 7, 1863...

Sawyer wrote a letter home, and read it aloud to the detective standing near. Upon coming to the last part of it, saying, 'Farewell, my dear wife, farewell, my children, farewell, mother,' he begged those standing by to excuse him, and turning aside, burst into tears. Flinn said he had no letter to write home, and only wanted a priest.

After writing this letter Captains Sawyer and Flinn were placed in close confinement, in a dungeon, underground. Here they were fed on corn bread and water, the dungeon being so damp that their clothing mildewed. When Sawyer's devoted wife received her husband's communication she immediately hastened to lay the matter before influential friends, and these at once proceeded to Washington and presented the case to the President.

My dear wife

I am under the necessity of informing you that my prospects look dark. This morning, all the Captains now in the prison at the Libby military prison, drew lots for two to be executed. It fell to my lot. Myself and Captain Flinn, of the Fifty-First Indiana Infantry, will be executed for two Captains executed by Burnside. The Provost General J. H. Winder, assures me that the Secretary of the War of the Southern Confederacy will permit yourself and my dear children to visit me before I am executed. You will be permitted to bring an attendant, Captain Whilldin, or uncle W.W. Ware, or Dan, had better come with you. My situation is hard to be borne, and I can not think of dying without seeing you and the children. You will be allowed to return without molestation to your home. I am resigned to whatever is in store for me, with the consolation that I die without having committed any crime. I have no trial, no jury, nor am I charged with any crime, but it fell to my lot.

You will proceed to Washington. My Government will give you transportation to Fortress Monroe, and you will get here by flag of truce, and return in the same way.

Bring with you a shirt for me. It will be necessary for you to preserve this letter, to bring evidence at Washington of my condition... My pay is due from the 21st of March, which you are entitled to. Captain B owes me fifty dollars, money lent to him when he went home on a furlough. You will write him at once, and he will send it to you.

My dear wife – the fortunes of war has put me in this position. If I must die, a sacrifice to my country,

VICTORIAN SERENITY
Above: Mary McKissick Sawyer, the Civil War hero's second wife, loved literature, music and art. She was a teacher and raised her two young boys as a single mother. She was a young widow, but never remarried after the death of her husband. He had sold the Chalfonte Hotel before meeting Mary.
Donlin collection

LOST A FATHER
Henry W. Sawyer II, at age three, with his brother Thomas Robb Sawyer, three months old. The boys were this age when their father, the Civil War hero, died suddenly in a Cape May pharmacy.
Donlin collection

with God's will I must submit; only let me see you once more, and I will die becoming a man and an officer, but for God's sake do not disappoint me. Write to me as soon as you get this, and go to Captain Whilldin, he will advise you what to do. I have done nothing to deserve this penalty. But you must submit to your fate. It will be no disgrace to myself, you or the children, but you may point with pride and say, 'I gave my husband,' my children will have the consolation to say, 'I was made an orphan for my country.' God will provide for you never fear. Oh! It is hard to leave you thus. I wish the ball that passed through my head in the last battle would have done its work; but it was not to be so... Write to me as soon as you get this; leave your letter open and I will get it... Farewell, farewell! and hope it is all for the best.

Remain yours until death.
H. W. Sawyer,
Captain first New Jersey Cavalry

The following letter was sent to Washington on July 15, 1863 by H. W. Halleck, General-in-Chief of Union forces, to Colonel Ludlow, Agent for Exchange of Prisoners of War:

The President directs that you immediately place General W. H. F. Lee and another officer selected by you not below the rank of captain, prisoners of war, in close confinement and under strong guard, and that you notify Mr. R. Ould, Confederate agent for exchange of prisoners of war, that if Capt. H. W. Sawyer, First New Jersey Volunteer Cavalry, and Captain John M. Flinn, Fifty-first Indiana Volunteers, or any other officers or men in the serve of the United States not guilty of crimes punishable with death by the laws of war, shall be executed by the enemy, the aforementioned prisoners will be immediately hung in retaliation. It is also directed that immediately on receiving official or other authentic information of the execution of Captain Sawyer and Captain Flinn, you will proceed to hang General Lee and the other rebel officer designated as herein above directed, and that you notify Robert Ould, Esq., of said proceeding and assure him that the Government of the United States will proceed to retaliate for every similarly barbarous violation of the laws of civilized war.

H.W. HALLECK
General-in-Chief

President Lincoln wrote and spoke, and action was immediate. General Lee, son of the Confederate Army Commander-in-Chief, Robert E. Lee, was placed in close confinement at

MAN ABOUT TOWN
Henry W. Sawyer owned several properties in Cape May and involved himself in politics and municipal projects. He had a gregarious personality and enjoyed gathering the news of the day on his rounds on foot and horseback. This portrait was taken shortly before his death on October 16, 1893.

PORTRAYING THE HERO
Dr Clark Donlin was fascinated by Sawyer's life, telling his story at Civil War Roundtables and portraying him on horseback at parades and school events. Dr Donlin, a Cape May Court House educator, attempted to make a museum of the 1859 home on Seashore Road where Sawyer lived in his later years with his wife Mary and two young sons. However, his efforts failed and the house was bulldozed July 10, 2000.
Donlin collection

Fort Monroe. The next day Captain Robert Tyler was placed in a Washington jail, the two held as hostages for Sawyer and Flinn. President Lincoln's order assured that the two Union captains were not executed. However, Sawyer and Flinn were left languishing in the miserable dungeon until August 16, when they were returned to the general prison population. Richmond newspapers continued to report that the two Yankee captains would be executed.

Negotiations continued through the winter and it wasn't until March, 1864 that Sawyer and Flinn won their release in an exchange that included Lee's son. Henry Washington Sawyer was free. Free at last! He had spent nine wretched months surviving in Libby Prison.

The reunion with his wife was in Trenton, at which time he was commissioned a major of his regiment. The couple traveled home to Cape May but, remarkably, it wasn't long before Sawyer, despite his wounds, capture and imprisonment, returned to the war. On August 31 he suffered two more minor wounds – at the Second Battle of Kernstown, Virginia. He recuperated and during the remainder of the war was stationed at the US Cavalry Headquarters in Washington, DC as an inspector of horses. He was honorably discharged May 24, 1865, and was welcomed to Cape May as a war hero.

His hotel experience began in 1867 when he became proprietor of the Ocean House in Cape May, a position he held until 1873. Sawyer was then recruited as manager of the new Clayton House hotel in Wilmington, Delaware and while there began designing a hotel of his own. He had already purchased a parcel at Howard and Sewell in Cape May, in 1872. He would call his dream The Chalfonte.

In 1876, with the construction of the new Chalfonte nearly complete, Sawyer bought the remainder of the square bounded by Columbia, Franklin, Sewell and Howard, with the exception of the corner of Howard and Columbia. Sawyer and his wife lived at the property while renting rooms.

Sawyer was a man of ritual – he rode around town on a white stallion, keeping up with news of the day. Mornings he climbed to his cupola with a view of the city and sea to watch the sun rise. Shortly after 7am, on the morning of November 9, 1878 he noticed smoke coming from the Ocean House on Perry Street. A worker spotted the fire, but newspapers reported it was Colonel Sawyer who sounded the alarm. Firefighting efforts failed and 11 hours later 35 acres of hotels and homes lay in smoking ruins – Cape May's worst-ever fire.

Flames did not reach the Chalfonte, two blocks beyond the fire boundary. The fire destroyed 2,000 hotel rooms, leaving only 200 in the city. Sawyer grasped the opportunity for more business – a year after the fire, builder D. D. Moore and Son added a 100-foot wing containing the dining room on the Sewell Avenue side. This addition is marked by a two-story colonnade in which changes in architectural detail are apparent. There is no evidence Sawyer had help from architects – he and his builders apparently designed the Chalfonte from Victorian pattern books used in that era by many local contractors.

The building is considered American Bracketed Villa, a stylistic hybrid. This style shares characteristics of the Italian Villa and Renaissance Revival but is in a category of its own. The Chalfonte is similar to a number of other architectural gems in Cape May – the Southern Mansion (the 1863 George Allen House), the Skinner home (the 1865 Neafie-Levy House), the Mainstay (the 1872 Jackson Clubhouse). Part of the Chalfonte's charm is that it evokes all

From The Archives

Henry Sawyer's obituary in the *Ocean Wave* newspaper from October, 1893...

Colonel Henry W. Sawyer, for many years proprietor of the Chalfonte hotel at Cape May City, dropped dead in Marcy & Mecray's drugstore at Cape May on Monday afternoon last.

Col. Sawyer was prominent in Grand Army circles, not only in South and West Jersey, but in the State Department as well. Colonel Sawyer fought in the war of the rebellion, and was recognized as one of the bravest soldiers that ever entered a battle. One of the most stirring incident of his life, and one which the Colonel loved to talk about, was his capture and confinement in Libby Prison, and his subsequent sentence to be shot to death, he having been the unfortunate victim of the drawing in the Lottery of Death.

The funeral took place yesterday afternoon with Masonic honors.

The late Colonel H. W. Sawyer was buried on Thursday of last week with civic and military honors, at Cold Spring Cemetery, Cape May. The funeral procession, which was a mile long, was the largest ever known at this end of the State. Rev. J. M. Cockins, Pastor of the Presbyterian Church, made an address on the public services of Colonel Sawyer. Masons and war veterans escorted his remains to the cemetery, where the impressive service ended with a volley of musketry, the roll of muffled drums and the bugle call taps.

sorts of descriptions, from an overgrown wedding cake to Steamboat Gothic, looking similar to a Mississippi riverboat with its vast stretches of jigsaw-decorated pillars, porches, brackets and balustrades. It is the most ornate and oldest continuously operating hotel in Cape May.

Sawyer sold the Chalfonte in 1888 after 13 years of ownership, one year before Harriet, his wife of 39 years, passed away.

New owners made extensions that added more rooms, as well as enlarging the dining room along Sewell Avenue in 1888 and again in 1895, bringing the number of rooms to 75.

Sawyer owned several other Cape May properties and became more active in local politics and community services. A lifelong Republican, he served three terms on Cape May City Council, was superintendent of New Jersey's Life Saving Stations and was an official greeter for Cape May – he introduced the celebrated John Philip Sousa Band at Congress Hall.

Despite his busy life, Sawyer was lonely after Harriet's death. He met a Philadelphia schoolteacher, Mary Emma McKissick, who was waitressing at a hotel in nearby Avalon. She was 27, he was 60. They married and had two sons. But their family life ended suddenly when Sawyer was stricken with a heart attack on October 16, 1893, at age 64. Thomas Robb Sawyer was just three months old, and Henry Washington Sawyer II was three.

The Civil War hero's funeral drew a cortege of wagons, carriages and horses more than a mile long. Sawyer is buried at the cemetery on Seashore Road at Cold Spring Church, where he was married to Harriet. The inscription on his tombstone reads: "A soldier whose deeds of valor and suffering for his country have been exceeded by no one. An officer of whom his men were justly proud."

By a strange quirk of fate, the hotel built by a Civil War hero of the north would be purchased by a daughter of the Confederacy who imposed a southern lifestyle that has sustained it for a century.

CHAPTER II

Southern Belle Goes North

*S*USIE, who was the first Satterfield to own the Chalfonte, was born April 12, 1861, the day the Civil War erupted at Fort Sumter, South Carolina. That was 150 years ago this year of 2011 and still the Chalfonte retains the southern roots instilled by Susie, the daughter of a Confederate general.

It was 4:30am, April 12 when a single 10-inch mortar burst over Fort Sumter. The red flare billowed 100 feet above the harbor and the sound boomed through the streets as the lovely antebellum city of Charlestown slept.

Tensions had been building. Fort Sumter was a Union garrison and President Lincoln, aware that provisions and troop spirits were running low, ordered an immediate expedition of food, supplies and manpower. Confederate General P. G. T. Beauregard heard help was on the way. The day before, he had sent two representatives aboard a rowboat, waving a white flag. Negotiations went on into the night, but

SOUTHERN GENTLEMAN
Lindsay Walker, a Confederate General, is the forefather of the Satterfields who owned and operated the Chalfonte for more than 60 years.
Phoebe Peyton Hanson

SUNDAY SOCIAL
Young people gathered at General Walker's Austin, Texas home for theater and musicales. Front row, third from left, Susie Walker and on her left, husband-to-be Calvin Satterfield. Back row, third from left: Mrs Walker (Sally Pleasants Elam), General Walker. Second from right: Lindsay "Tyee" Walker and to her right, the famous short story writer O. Henry, who had a crush on her.
Phoebe Peyton Hanson

Union Major Robert Anderson refused to abandon Sumter.

Before dawn on the 12th, General Beauregard ordered the Confederacy's first shot at the fort. The Union answered with a volley of fire. Cannon and musket fire exploded across the harbor. The sky lit up. Fires erupted. Smells of the inferno mixed with the scents of spring flowering jasmine and magnolias. Charleston citizens lined streets and verandas along the harbor to watch the firefight, unaccustomed to the sights and thunder of war.

The battle raged for 34 hours until mid-day April 13, when the Union troops raised a white flag and began evacuating. Not a life had been lost on either side.

The next day President Lincoln called for 75,000 volunteers to face off the Confederate insurgency. Southern leaders didn't expect an all-out war when they seceded from the Union two months earlier, a conflict that would change their way of life forever.

The little girl born the first day of the war was nicknamed Sumter, in recognition of the Confederate victory at the fort, although her baptized name was Susan. Her parents were of the Virginia landed gentry whose plantations dotted the lush landscape from Gordonsville to

The little girl born the first day of the war was nicknamed Sumter, in recognition of the Confederate victory at the fort, although her baptized name was Susan... The family's joy over baby Sumter, though, soon turned to uneasiness when word spread of Lincoln's call to arms.

Charlottesville. The Walkers' estate at Point of Fork, south of Richmond, lay at the junction of the James and Rivanna Rivers.

Susie's father, Reuben Lindsay Walker (1827-1890), graduated from the prestigious Virginia Military Institute in 1845. Her mother, Sally Pleasants Elam, was a granddaughter of Virginia Governor James Pleasants.

The family's joy over baby Sumter, though, soon turned to uneasiness when word spread of Lincoln's call to arms.

Reuben Lindsay Walker became one of the first to volunteer in Virginia, accepting command of the First Company of Artillery – the Purcell Battery. The troops organized within a week and left Richmond for the Potomac River at Aquia Creek. Their mission was to protect the budding spring countryside from Union gunboats.

Walker had been a top student at VMI, earning a degree in engineering. He was extraordinarily handsome and tall for the time, at six-foot-four. He wore a full mustache and clipped beard and rode and strode with posture and pride in his battle grays. There are many references to Walker being the "handsomest soldier in the Confederacy." Despite his mannerly way of the Virginia gentry and his good looks, he

was called "Old Rube" for Reuben. He disliked the nickname and preferred to be addressed as R. Lindsay Walker.

Walker led a celebrated military career with the Artillery of Northern Virginia. He engaged in 63 battles and four horses were shot from under him – yet he was never wounded.

This excerpt from the book *General A.P. Hill: The Story of a Confederate Soldier,* by James I. Robertson Jr, says this about Walker:

The man selected to command the nine artillery batteries in Hill's division was awesome-looking Maj. Reuben Lindsay Walker. Eight years older than Hill and descended from another prominent Virginia family, Lindsay Walker stood six feet four inches tall. He had long hair, a sweeping mustache, and an imperial beard. Piercing black eyes stared from a face with a habitually grave expression. No other artillerist in Confederate service had more organizational skill than Walker. He participated in sixty-three engagements without suffering injury. After the war, whenever someone asked Walker if he had been wounded, he would draw himself up and reply: "No sir, and it was not my fault!"

Walker was in charge of the Artillery Corps at the battles of Richmond, Warrenton Springs, Manassas Junction, Second Manassas, Harper's Ferry, Snicker's Ferry, Fredericksburg and others in 1882. He was promoted to Colonel of the Artillery in 1863, engaging at Chancellorsville, Gettysburg, Ainesville, Bristoe Station, Rixeyville, among others. Battles in 1864 included Spottsylvania, Jericho Ford, Petersburg, Squirrel Level Road and Jarrat's Depot.

In January, 1865 he was made Brigadier Gen-

SOUTHERN BELLES

Left: Susie Pleasants Walker at age 20 in 1881 – she married Calvin Satterfield five years later. Susie was known for her fire, wit and unbridled energy. She met Calvin, from a wealthy Maryland family, in Austin, Texas, where he was a newspaper editor. Center: Daughter Rose, pictured in 1906, had just graduated from Hollins Institute and was engaged to be married. Susie threw a party for the young couple on a James River boat – but the night ended in tragedy when a freak accident caused both to drown. Susie descended into deep grief and bought the Chalfonte to give her life a renewed purpose. Right: Susie's daughter Phoebe in 1916, a year before her wedding at the Chalfonte. She enjoyed the social whirl of the Avant-Garde era, but had no taste for the back-breaking work at the hotel.
Phoebe Peyton Hanson
Hollins University Archives

CITY ON FIRE
Opposite: Susie was born the night Fort Sumter, in Charleston, was attacked by Confederate forces.
Library of Congress

eral in command of the Third Artillery Corps and dispatched in advance of General Robert E. Lee's column toward Appomattox Station, Virginia. Four Confederate supply trains awaited Lee's forces. The cars carried clothing, blankets, ammunition, medical supplies and food. Walker arrived with 100 cannons, 200 baggage wagons and an army hospital wagon. Walker's soldiers were settling for the night, cooking supper, and Walker was sitting on a stump getting a shave, when the cry of 'Yankees!' went up.

Walker's men, guarding the supply train, fired shots over Appomattox Station. They had no idea that Union General George Custer, learning of the supply train, had hurried his men ahead. Walker was surprised to find Union cavalry nearby and mounted an immediate defense. Although Walker pushed back the first two assaults with artillery canisters, the third thrust, at night, under a full moon, overwhelmed his forces. Custer's cavalry captured 24 cannons, 200 wagons and 1,000 ragged prisoners. It was the beginning of the end for the Confederacy. Robert E. Lee surrendered his hungry and worn army the next day.

The Confederacy defeated, General Walker returned to his family at Point of Fork on May 5, 1865. His little girl Sumter was now four years old and General Walker was 38. He tried to return to plantation life but it was physically and financially impossible. That lifestyle had been lost with the war.

The Walkers were one of the early patrician families of Virginia in Colonial times. Walker

Baltimore Inn, Cape May, N. J.

was the great-grandson of Dr Thomas Walker (1715-1794), an explorer, neighbor and guardian of Thomas Jefferson after Jefferson's father died. Dr Walker's prized plantation, Castle Hill, remains today at the foot of the Southwest Mountains near President Jefferson's Monticello and the city of Charlottesville. Through his marriage to young widow Mildred Thornton Meriwether in 1741 Dr Walker acquired 15,000 acres. The Albermarle County Inventory List showed 86 slaves, 93 cattle, 22 horses and two carriages.

In 1764 Dr Walker designed and built Castle Hill, a clapboard Colonial residence. The home's great square hall was scene of historic soirees. A youthful, music-loving Thomas Jefferson played the violin there, while James Madison danced into the night. Jefferson, a neighbor, was a frequent visitor. Six presidents were among the guest book's VIPs: George Washington, James Monroe, Andrew Jackson, James Buchanan, Martin Van Buren, John Tyler, Patrick Henry,

SUSIE'S FIRST HOTEL
Calvin and Susie Satterfield moved to Philadelphia after daughter Rose's drowning. *The Philadelphia Inquirer* **social notes reported they lived in Germantown and summered in Cape May. Susie managed the Baltimore Inn, above, before buying the Chalfonte.**
Don Pocher

GRANDMA AND GRANDPA
Next page: That is the title of this photograph in a family album. The Satterfields had moved back to Virginia from Philadelphia, residing in Richmond in the winter. Their staff remained loyal and joined them for the trek to Cape May and the Chalfonte.
Phoebe Peyton Hanson

Robert E. Lee, Henry Clay and Daniel Webster.

The original Castle Hill remains today as a National Historic Landmark.

All of this glamorous history mattered little in the reconstruction days after the war. R. Lindsay Walker gave up with regret the planter's lifestyle his family had enjoyed for more than 100 years, although his engineering degree from VMI served him well in a new career as a railroad official and later as construction supervisor of the new Texas capitol building in Austin from 1882 to 1888.

The Walkers lived near the construction site, their home offering Virginia-style hospitality and an opportunity for young men to court Susie, in her 20s, and her younger sister Lindsay. There were picnics, parlor musicales, horseback riding, Sunday excursions into the country. Calvin Satterfield was new to Austin, too, and was among the young men who were attracted to the spirited Walker sisters. He was from Maryland and headed to Austin to work at the

Daily Statesman. He covered the construction of the capitol for the newspaper and became acquainted with the Walker family, Susie in particular.

Phoebe Peyton Hanson *Born 1921, San Antonio, Texas; Susie's granddaughter and daughter of Phoebe Satterfield Peyton* "Grandmother and Calvin Satterfield [1861-1936] had Virginia in common, but met in Texas. He was a University of Virginia law graduate and located in Texas to become managing editor of Austin's *Daily Statesman.* The young Walker ladies apparently were quite social. There are family stories that the famous writer O. Henry was a guest at their home and courted my aunt Tyee, whose name was Lindsay. He was said to be bashful, but smitten with Tyee."

Calvin Satterfield grew up in Greensborough (now Greensboro), Maryland. His father, William C. Satterfield (1822-1896) taught school and ran a store before he joined the gold rush to California. He found no fortune in gold and returned home to become a wealthy man. He had a mercantile business on the Choptank River, ran schooners that traded in the West Indies and South America, owned five thousand acres of farmland, milled timber and was a preeminent grower of peaches. His wife, Phoebe Allen, was a granddaughter of Ethan Allen of Vermont and Green Mountain Boys fame. Charged as a traitor by the British, Allen was freed in a prisoner exchange. He later was accused of treason, but was never charged because his mission to force the Continental Congress to recognize Vermonters' land claims was upheld in court.

Phoebe Peyton Hanson "Grandmother and Grandfather were married June 30th, 1886. [Susie's obituary states they were wed in Greensboro, Maryland.] The next year Grandfather was appointed Texas Post Office Inspector. Some time later, they returned to Grandfather's home in Maryland to help with the family business before settling eventually in Virginia. They raised four children: Rose, Fred, Phoebe and Calvin Jr.

"Rose, the eldest, had just graduated from Hollins Institute in 1906. Rose was the star of the family. She was the smartest, the most beautiful. Susie was very proud of her. Rose was engaged to be married, and Susie arranged a party on a boat on the James River near Richmond. That night changed lives forever."

O. Henry's Girl

▨ Celebrated short story writer O. Henry (1862-1910) moved to Texas in 1882 from his native Greensboro, North Carolina to help combat a persistent cough. Back then he was known as William Sidney Porter, a bon vivant in young social circles enjoying music and theater at home salons. O. Henry was a pen name invented when the writer was first achieving fame for his style of surprise endings. In Austin, Texas he took a fancy to Lindsay "Tyee" Satterfield, pictured above with friend and fellow equestrian, Julian Morris. The famous writer and Tyee socialized on several occasions. *Phoebe Peyton Hanson*

Helena Lefroy Caperton *(1878-1962) Editor of* Social Record of Virginia, *from her 1940s booklet, 'The Chalfonte'* "One moonlit summer night, Mrs Satterfield took a party of young people in a small launch down the James River for an evening's picnic. Her young daughter was among those who sang to the accompaniment of a banjo and guitar. During the evening Rose and a young man climbed up to sit on the roof that covered the cockpit of the launch. Still later in that evening the lights of the side-wheeler Pocahontas, the steamer that plied between Old Point Comfort and Richmond, were sighted. The wash from her stern rocked the small vessel precariously, but the laughter and the singing continued, stimulated by blasts from the steamer's whistle. In the darkness and confusion of merriment, there was no hint of tragedy, as the launch continued on its way. When it reached its destination, horror fell upon them. Rose and the young man were gone. They had been swept overboard by the wash from the passing steamer Pocahontas, and in the darkness, and because of the gay singing, their cries for help had not been heard. That was all, all but the solemn booming of the gun that at last brought to the surface of the river all that was left of the youth and beauty and love.

"Such an unspeakable bereavement would have caused the average mother to retreat from normal living or go into permanent shock, but Susan Pleasants Satterfield was not average, but a character of determination, fire and wit.

"Susan Satterfield bought the Chalfonte not with the idea of profit, but because she wanted hard work, so that she would be able to submerge a devastating loss with labor. Labor so unremitting that at last the blessing of sleep might come to her."

Susie could not get over losing Rose. The tragedy devastated her. She set about to lose herself in the loss of Rose.

The belles of Richmond and their families had a long tradition of summering in Cape May. In the days before the Civil War, wealthy Virginia planters traveled by steamboat, bringing with them servants, even their horses and carriages, to make statements of ego and wealth on the beachfront. Later families traveled by train to Philadelphia and transferred to Cape May, or they caught a ferry in Delaware and sailed across the bay to the resort city. Lost in her grief, Susie decided to get away from Richmond,

move to Philadelphia and vacation in Cape May.

Nancy Satterfield Davey *Born 1926, Richmond, Virginia, Susie's granddaughter and daughter of Mary "Meenie" Morris and Calvin Satterfield Jr*

"Susie was befriended by the Storey sisters who owned the Baltimore Inn – the large hotel with turrets – on Jackson Street. [The Baltimore Inn was built following the 1878 fire and razed in the urban renewal of the late 1960s.] The sisters complained they were getting too old to operate the hotel. After staying there a couple seasons, Susie stepped up to the challenge and agreed to manage the inn. She was a natural. She was successful. She decided she liked running a hotel."

IN HER GLORY
Susie Satterfield directs a touring car festooned with flowers and occupied by three young ladies. Husband Calvin is barely visible under the Chalfonte porch awnings.
Satterfield family collection

BOARDWALK OUTING
Granddaughter Sally Jackson takes Susie for a trip in her highback wicker wheelchair. Note the Stockton Hotel in the background.
Mead family collection

The Chalfonte had floundered through about six owners and a couple sheriff sales in the 1890s. It was in poor condition, but Susie Satterfield fell in love with the place. Its lace woodwork, tall columns, wide verandas, long halls, high windows, shutters and louvers, formal fireplaces, library, music room, long, narrow dining room, spoke to her of the antebellum plantation homes she knew that survived the war. It was an emotional, compulsive move. Susie and Calvin Satterfield bought the hotel from Hannah Cresse and opened it in 1911.

The compound then as now included the hotel, the 1910 Howard Street Cottage, the

1868 Annex, a "railroad" house, moved to the grounds, the 1870 Franklin Street Cottage, the Quarters, where the African-American help stayed, and the Laundry. In the 1920s, the Tin House was added.

Phoebe Peyton Hanson "Oh, there was a lot of work. Susie's daughter, my mother Phoebe, they called her Big Phoebe, even though she was petite, said they worked very hard. Mother told of making screens, many screens for those big windows. All members of the family had major projects. Mother was not in love with the Chalfonte. For her it was labor and not a labor of love."

Helena Lefroy Caperton "It is infinitely touching to contemplate the fact that, rising

HIGH WATER
A flood disables a laundry truck in 1919. It wasn't the first or last time the hotel was hit by Mother Nature.
Satterfield family collection

SUMMER PAL
Right: Chalfonte staffer Cayton in 1921 with Susie Satterfield's granddaughter, Little Phoebe Peyton, who remembers tagging after Cayton as a child.
Phoebe Peyton Hanson

above her desolation, this mother [Susie Satterfield] created this sanctuary of relaxation and happiness for so many in the years to come. With no larger experience than any lady gains when running her own household, Mrs. Satterfield bought the Chalfonte. The place gloomed under the melancholy décor of dark woodwork and furniture upholstered in black horsehair. Upstairs there was only one closet for the many bedrooms and one bathroom. Today [the 1940s], the impression is that of a large but simple and well run country house, done in pastel colors, white paint and gay chintz, good lighting and a well-stocked library.

"Fine antiques furnish the lobby, but there is

FAMILY SNAPSHOT
Calvin III and Meenie Satterfield with daughter Nancy and son Calvin IV, better known as Sat, dressed up in Cape May, circa 1929.
Phoebe Peyton Hanson

no feeling of its being a hotel lobby. There is a roll top desk in one corner, the only concession to business. Around it are comfortable chairs usually occupied by guests, chatting with which ever member of the Satterfield family happens to be on duty. There is a small showcase for cigarettes, candy and stamps. Even this concession to commerce is camouflaged by a delicate Victorian sofa placed in front of it. There are always lovely arrangements of flowers from the gardens which, thanks to the sea air and sun, are a riot of bloom all summer long. The deep shaded porches are cool, and swept by Atlantic breezes, no matter how hot the weather, and it is here that guests are reunited, year after year. They are joyously welcomed as the Philadelphia crowd, the Baltimore crowd, and the Richmond crowd."

Susie Satterfield ruled with manners, punctuality, a sense of humor and tight-fisted management inherited from her gene pool of cul-

tured Virginia country folk who had refined a leisured grace of lifestyle. She imported the staff from Richmond and North Carolina. They were African-Americans who remained devoted to continuing their generations of service intimately, hands-on, one family to another. The Satterfields transformed the Chalfonte, built by a northern cavalry hero, into a retreat of southern hospitality; the sort of place that had been ruined in the war. Susie favored the Edwardian style of dress fashionable among women in business. She wore jackets with broad shoulders and long skirts in dark colors, with soft blouses and modest jewelry.

Phoebe Peyton Hanson "I spent most of my summers at the Chalfonte. The Satterfields stayed in the family wing, on the Howard Street side, far left and up the steps. We all shared one very large bathroom with no windows. We took turns taking baths before dressing for dinner. I remember getting up once, and leaving the

dinner table – I was about nine – and grand-mother Susie called me back, and spoke to me and asked me to start over, and leave the room properly. She was very strict about manners. Meals were eaten at big family tables. My children and grandchildren all ate in the Children's Dining Room until they were six or seven years old."

Nancy Satterfield Davey "Susie had a very strong personality. She wore the pants. When she would fix you with those eyes she meant business. She was very strong and very petite. I believe she was under five feet tall. She had a wonderful personality. People were drawn to her. She was very funny. She told good jokes. In later years, she and my father would team up telling jokes. They had a comedy give-and-take that was quite hilarious. Some of Susie's jokes were passed down through family from antebellum times. In her older years, Susie was a feature around Cape May and Richmond being pushed in her high-back wheelchair. She had become crippled up from arthritis and Helen, who would become the Chalfonte's famous cook, was her nurse. She pushed Susie all over town in that big wheelchair, wicker with high wheels. Susie still

GUYS AND GALS
Opposite page, top: The Satterfield sisters, Lindsay, left, and Phoebe, being courted on the Chalfonte porch in 1916. Phoebe would be married at the hotel the following year.

PLAY TIME
Opposite page, bottom: Susie Satterfield's grandchildren, from left to right, Tommy and Phoebe Peyton, Calvin III, aka Sat, and Jimmy Satterfield at Stockton Bathhouse in the early 1920s.

BABES OF SUMMER
Above: Grandmother Susie Satterfield with Phoebe Peyton and Calvin III Satterfield and the nurse who would become the Chalfonte's famous chef, Helen Dickerson. Helen's Chalfonte experience began when she was three years old, helping Susie pick flowers for the dining tables.

SLEEP OVER
Right: Susie Satterfield allowed her daughters to host a party with girlfriends soon after the family opened the hotel in 1911. Lindsay is second from left and Phoebe is far right.
Phoebe Peyton Hanson

had a strong sense of humor. She would hold court on the porch. She was a very funny lady.

"I was at the Chalfonte every year from the time I was two months old. So I have summered there for more than 80 years. We had so much fun there. The same families gathered every year from Louisville, Pittsburgh, Philadelphia, Baltimore. They kept coming back, from one generation to another, just as we Satterfields did. The Chalfonte was a magnet for us; a time when we put our cares aside and played and partied. Maybe we partied too much. I liked it better in the old days when we set up the bar in the Play Room, now the Henry Sawyer Room, before the King Edward Bar.

"The Depression years were tough. My father had another Chalfonte, a winter resort at Pinehurst, North Carolina. It had the same southern influence as the Cape May Chalfonte. The same sort of food. It was a winter time place with golf, polo games, horseback riding. I went there last when I was seven. We lost the Chalfonte at Pinehurst in the Depression."

Susie's son, Calvin Jr (Nancy's father), and his wife Meenie were about to lose the Cape May Chalfonte as well. They had taken over ownership in 1921. A sheriff sale loomed in 1933, but Susie came to the rescue and put up $300 to keep it in the family. Although her health was failing and arthritis forced her into a wheelchair, she continued to spend summers at the Chalfonte, entertaining guests with her stories.

Susie Satterfield died in Richmond the day after Christmas, 1939. Her obituary noted she was born the day the Civil War started and that her nickname was Sumter. Now World War II headlines were worrying her family as the year ended with Russia bombing Helsinki, the Nazis gaining control of Poland, and meat rationing beginning in Britain.

Susie had been queen of the Chalfonte for 28 years. Determined not to let the hotel pass to strangers, Calvin Jr and Meenie bought it back from Susie's estate and began another era that lasted for more than 40 years.

BEACH CHIC
Swimsuit fashions circa 1930 modeled before a dip in the Atlantic by Bill Bethel, Susie Satterfield's daughter Lindsay, Meenie and Calvin Satterfield III.
Phoebe Peyton Hanson

CHAPTER III

Satterfields Are Here To Stay

THE 1940 season arrived with the Satterfield family dynamic about to change. Kin and staff were still mourning the death of the matriarch, Susie Satterfield, the Christmas just passed. As Memorial Day approached, the Chalfonte shutters opened, the awnings lifted… and war worries descended.

Headlines announced British fighters and the German Luftwaffe engaging in fights over France. The Nazis entrapped troops in the French port of Dunkirk and, miraculously, thousands of British troops escaped in an armada of small boats. Soon the worsening war would alter life for the Satterfields.

This would be the last season that Calvin Satterfield Jr and his sons Calvin III (Sat) and James (Jimmy) would enjoy some relaxing summer days together. Calvin III would be a senior that fall at his father's alma mater, the Virginia Military Institute. Jimmy would be a junior at VMI. They were the third generation to attend

MILITARY TRADITION
Calvin Satterfield Jr (left) in his 1913 graduation photo from the Virginia Military Institute. He served in the field artillery in World War I. His son, Calvin "Sat" Satterfield III (right), graduated from VMI in 1941. Sat's brother Jimmy, also a VMI graduate, entered combat in the South Pacific in 1942.
VMI archives

THE MAN IN WHITE
Previous page: Calvin Satterfield Sr on the running board of his 1920s-era touring car. Calvin had a reputation for being impeccably dressed in white linen, white bucks and bow tie. The roadster sometimes was used to transport moonshine from the winter Chalfonte in North Carolina to the summer Chalfonte in Cape May.
Satterfield family collection

the military school.

Sat graduated in 1941 and was called to serve in the Third Army under General George Patton in Europe. Jimmy graduated the next year and within 10 days he was on his way with the cavalry to Fort Riley, Kansas and the South Pacific under General Douglas McArthur. Three of Jimmy's roommates also shipped out, but only Jimmy survived.

The health of the boys' father, Calvin Junior, was declining. He was not his usual humorous, commanding self. For years he had lent mirth and panache to the place. Dressed daily in a freshly pressed white linen suit, he greeted and entertained guests on the Chalfonte verandas.

One of his favorite yarns happened during his VMI days. He was riding Colonel Wise's horse Gunga Din. The stead got spooked and bolted, with him hanging on the saddle at regimental review – scattering the band, breaking up the formations, scaring other horses, cadets and infuriating the command. Gunga Din galloped off toward a cliff and Satterfield, fearing for his life, grabbed his saber with both hands, and somehow reined in the horse, saving both from going over the cliff.

TIN HOUSE PARTY
Sally Jackson, second from right in the front row, was a key Chalfonte staffer in the early 1940s. She had a magnetic personality, a quick wit and a knack for pulling together impromptu parties like this one. On the far right is Henry "Hutch" Hutchinson.
Mead family collection

The summer of 41, Meenie was caring for her sick husband, worried about her sons and assuming more responsibility for managing the Chalfonte, with help from family members and friends. Her husband was convalescing at Cliveden, a guest house across the street, protected from the chaos of closing the hotel for the season. Arrangements were being made for him to return to Richmond, but a week after Labor Day, on September 8, Calvin Satterfield Jr died suddenly. He was only 49 years old. Some family members attributed his short life to flu and breathing poisons during World War I when he was a captain in the Field Artillery.

Daughter Nancy says her father and friends drank awful stuff in prohibition and the brew was not conducive to good health. He had bootleggers in Pinehurst, North Carolina and Cape May, where in those days, Nancy says, the fishmonger and bootlegger were one and the same.

Meenie sometimes drove up from the winter Chalfonte at Pinehurst with a keg of moonshine in the rear of her roadster. There was the memorable trip when Meenie was driving through Washington, DC, with Jimmy (and the keg) in the back. He got car sick, the keg sprang a leak, and Meenie, taking side roads and fearing jail time if caught, kept driving straight through to the Chalfonte. No one remembers if there was anything left in the keg.

The Chalfonte's survival has a habit of resting on the shoulders of women. Following the footsteps of her mother-in-law Susie, Mary (Meenie) Morris Satterfield chose to continue running the Chalfonte after her husband's death, at a time when her sons were on the battlefield. She managed the hotel for three decades with imagination, hard work, charm, wit, patience, the support of an extended family and the dedicated skills of an African-American staff. "Sweet" is the adjective used by some family and staff to describe Meenie. Daughter Nancy says she sugar-coated unruly, outrageous situations but that underneath was a steel magnolia, if not

THE AGE OF THE AUTO
By the 1930s and 40s, more families were preferring the automobile to the train for their trips to the Chalfonte. Pictured is the Sewell Avenue façade and the Franklin Street Cottage, with its Carribean-style propped-up shutters.
Satterfield family collection

by design, by necessity.

Meenie had a partner in Helen Young Horsley Dickerson, who started at the hotel as a babysitter when she herself was still a child, and then became Susie Satterfield's nurse. Helen worked as a waitress and then ran the dining room, but she was coming into her own in the kitchen. When the cook got sick, Helen was asked to take over temporarily – instead, she remained head cook for nearly 40 years. She possessed managerial skills and was a gifted cook who perfected the Virginia foods that had become tradition. Most of all, she was loyal and never faltered in her dedication to the Chalfonte – its kitchen, guests and the Satterfield family.

Meenie was an unlikely hotel proprietor. She was a Richmond society girl, the daughter of an Episcopal minister, Dr James W. Morris, who was a missionary in Brazil around 1900 and again from 1920 until 1926. She was born in Brazil, where her father had met her mother, Stella Tweedy, the daughter of a British railroad entrepreneur. Meenie attended Saint Catherine's, school of the elite in Richmond, and it is

SWEET MOMENT
Left: Meenie Satterfield, who loved summer hats, and older son Calvin III.
Satterfield family collection

THE MATRIARCH
Above: Meenie's portrait hangs over the fireplace in the Chalfonte lobby. Her daughter-in-law Maria commissioned it from Joe Court, a member of a family which has vacationed at the hotel for almost 100 years.
Photo by John Lynner Peterson

HERE'S NANCY!
Opposite: In freckles and pigtails, Nancy Satterfield is caught on camera in the 1930s. She has spent more than 80 summers at the Chalfonte and is a wonderful story-teller, full of wit, with a great memory.
Satterfield family collection

there that she earned her nickname. She tended to quickly emphasize the three Ms – Mary Minor Morris – when asked her name, and she was often asked to repeat it. A friend said, "Oh, eenie, meenie, minie, mo," and the meenie stuck. She was for the rest of her life Meenie.

Meenie and Calvin's daughter Nancy was 15 when her father died and her brothers Sat and Jimmy went off to war. She says that as youngsters the boys made up games. Sat was always the hero, Jimmy the villain and she the victim, rescued always.

Nancy Satterfield Davey "My brothers were members of the Greatest Generation. Mother and I agonized over their safety. We were nervous every day waiting for the mail. Letters from the front, infrequent, were cherished. The good news about wartime was that it was a busy time at the Chalfonte, and profitable for my mother. Her brother Jimmy Morris had auditing and organizational skills. He set up a bookkeeping system, handled the accounts, organized a room's layout and reservations system. The hotel filled with military families, many from

Post Card

CORRESPONDENCE

Dear Mrs. Vanderslice,

We were very disappointed to find that you all will not be able to come to the Chalfonte this year but certainly hope that you will come again soon.

Please my very best to Mrs. Meredith and my very best wishes to you.

Sincerely,
Mary M. Satterfield
(Mrs. Calvin)

July sixth -

ADDRESS

Mrs. John A. Vanderslice
218 Vineyard Road
Harrisburg, Pennsylvania

---

the Wildwood Naval Air Station. They shared their rations with the hotel kitchen. Anne LeDuc (who later owned the Chalfonte) and I were desk clerks. Martha Nash joined Mother in running the hotel. Both were widowed at a young age. Their husbands had been schoolmates at VMI. Martha was a tiny person with a big personality and giant help to my mother. She was in charge of the laundry, sending it out, counting every sheet and wash cloth. The war years were an interesting time at the hotel. Our family was scattered in military service, but at home our family rallied to keep the hotel running, and the Chalfonte remained the family compass."

Susan Farris Jackson *Born 1934, Kingsport, Tennessee, granddaughter of Susie Satterfield, daughter of Fred Satterfield (1899-1989)* "I visited the Chalfonte the first time in 1941 when I was seven. My father, Fred Satterfield, Susie's son, sent my mother and me home from Manila, knowing war was inevitable. My father, after Virginia Military Institute, worked for the National City Bank of New York, the Asian division.

"He sold his car and house and was sitting in a hotel waiting for his plane to leave when Pearl

MISS YOU ALREADY
Above: This postcard, from Mary Satterfield, illustrates the relationship the hotel management had with its guests, one that remains to this day.

FAMILY GATHERING
Opposite above: Maria Carter Satterfield, husband Calvin III, his mother Meenie, his sister Nancy, and Dot Walker, a Satterfield cousin.

PORCH TIME
Opposite below: Calvin Satterfield in his signature bow tie with one of the family youngsters. Calvin and his mother Susie had a porch comedy routine that tickled Chalfonte guests in the days of homemade entertainment.
Satterfield family collection

Harbor was attacked. He was taken a civilian prisoner of war and held captive until the end of the war. Mother died when I was 11, in January of 1945. She died not knowing if Father was dead or alive. She did not know his welfare and whereabouts all through the war. My father came home in April of 45, and he did not know that his wife, my mother, had died.

"Father and I vacationed at the Chalfonte every year long after the war. I was in boarding school in Virginia, and in summer, with my mother gone, I stayed with different family members. I lived out of a suitcase. In my teen years I summered at the Chalfonte with Meenie Satterfield as my guardian. I was a pretty wild 16-year-old. Meenie had a lot of patience with me. She was very good at running the hotel, a great hostess, and excellent with the staff.

"Theodore, who could do anything, was among the staff that my grandmother Susie had brought up from Virginia. He handled a lot of maintenance and in the kitchen carved the roast beef and lamb. Theodore took me fishing off the jetty. I tagged along with Dot and Lucille in old tennis shoes, to go crabbing in the marshes.

From The Archives

From the *Richmond News Leader* on September 19, 1917...

Rev. and Mrs James W. Morris announce the engagement of their daughter, Mary Minor, to Captain Calvin Satterfield Jr, son of Mr and Mrs Calvin Satterfield of Washington, formerly of this city. The wedding will be celebrated on the morning of October 6th, at 10:30 o'clock in historic Monumental Church of which the bride's father is rector, and Dr Morris will perform the ceremony.

Miss Morris, who is a lovely girl, made her formal bow to Richmond society two seasons ago, and has been an acknowledged belle of the younger society set. Captain Satterfield, who is a grandson of the late General Lindsay Walker, is captain and adjutant of the First Battalion, First Regiment, Virginia Field Artillery, and was an honor graduate of the Virginia Military Institute, where he was a distinguished cadet officer. Both Miss Morris and Captain Satterfield belong to old and well-known Southern families and their wedding this fall will be an important society event.

OUR GAL SAL
Left: Sally Jackson was the Satterfield family show girl. She sang, danced, loved high drama and hijinx. Here she performs some gymnastics at the beach with a friend, while cousin Jimmy Satterfield looks on.
Mead family collection

THREE'S COMPANY
Opposite: Sally Jackson Mead, her mother Lindsay and Lindsay's brother Fred Satterfield. Fred was a banker in Hawaii, and was taken a Japanese prisoner of war after Pearl Harbor. His daughter Susan Farris Jackson spent wartime summers at the Chalfonte under the guidance of her aunt Meenie until her father came home from prison camp.
Mead family collection

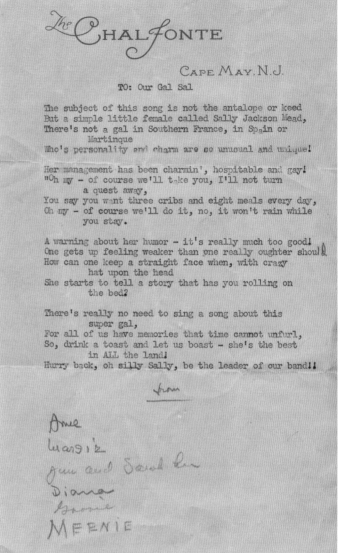

The subject of this song is not the antelope or keed
But a simple little female called Sally Jackson Mead,
There's not a gal in Southern France, in Spain or
        Martinque
Who's personality and charm are so unusual and unique!

Her management has been charmin', hospitable and gay!
"Oh my - of course we'll take you, I'll not turn
        a quest away,
You say you want three cribs and eight meals every day,
Oh my - of course we'll do it, no, it won't rain while
        you stay.

A warning about her humor - it's really much too good!
One gets up feeling weaker than one really ougher shoul
How can one keep a straight face when, with crazy
        hat upon the head
She starts to tell a story that has you rolling on
        the bed?

There's really no need to sing a song about this
        super gal,
For all of us have memories that time cannot unfurl,
So, drink a toast and let us boast - she's the best
        in ALL the land!
Hurry back, oh silly Sally, be the leader of our band!!

from

Anne
Margie
Jim and Sarah Lou
Diana
Goonie
MEENIE

They were a little older than I, daughters of Helen Dickerson, the cook, who took excellent care of me. Helen was wonderful, strong and beautiful and a lovely person. Meenie could lean on Helen. She relied on Helen a lot.

"Helen's mother Clementine was a chambermaid. She was round and short and always with a grin on her face, a little barrel of a person, and a barrel of fun. At night, when the workday had been closed down, when the breezes came up, the staff gathered by the laundry room… and sang. I can hear the songs now, old ballads. My favorite was:

Gonna take a Sentimental Journey,
Gonna set my heart at ease.
Gonna make a Sentimental Journey,
to renew old memories.

Never thought my heart could be so yearny.
Why did I decide to roam?

OLD SOUTH SOCIETY
Sally Jackson in a cotillion gown, circa 1939, at Sweet Briar College, where she participated in Plantation Day. Right: A song written by Meenie Satterfield and the Chalfonte staff, bidding farewell to Sally, who was taking leave of her hotel duties.

PLAY TIME
Opposite: Sally Jackson's husband, Ernest "Boots" Mead, a serious musician, was fun loving and so in love with Sally. They met at the Chalfonte the summer of 1943 and were married in 1949.
Mead family collection

Gotta take that Sentimental Journey,
Sentimental Journey home.
Sentimental Journey.

"That song said it for me about the Chalfonte and still does. In recent years, my family [three children and nine grandchildren] have gone to the Satterfield family reunions every three years at the Chalfonte. I love the Chalfonte. I have crawled every nook and cranny of the place. It is part of me. A special place of fun and protection. The Chalfonte has always loved me back."

Ernest "Boots" Campbell Mead Jr *Born 1918, Charlottesville, Virginia; Professor Emeritus of Music, University of Virginia; husband of the late Sally Lindsay Jackson (1920-1989); granddaughter of Susie Satterfield* "In the summer of 1943, my mother had died. She had been a very good friend, a confidante, of Calvin Satterfield's wife Meenie, who was running the Chalfonte at the time. Meenie

very sweetly thought she would invite me up to the Chalfonte. She was concerned about me. I am in Richmond, and how do I get to the tip of New Jersey. I had to take a train from Richmond and leave at 6am for Philadelphia, and transfer to another train, and arrive at Cape May at 7:25 in the evening. Traveling was not first class, it was Tunaville Trolley style. Meenie kindly met me at the train station, and driving me to the Chalfonte, she said, 'Oh, the dining room closes at 7:30, so I cannot give you any dinner. You can go into the village and get something. We will go to the Chalfonte and get you squared away.'

"On entering, Meenie said, 'Oh, we are full. But I will put you in the cupola.' Now, the cupola sits on top of the roof, accessible only by steep stairs from the third floor. Up the steep stairs and there is this little room, with a single bed, and four high windows, and the bath is down the steep steps to the third floor. Oh, my, I thought, this is an unusual accommodation. I came to love the cupola room. There's a view of all of Cape May and the beach.

"So this first summer's evening at the Chalfonte, I wash up and went down to the lobby, and at the side exit, I see this very attractive young woman, and she introduced herself and it was Sally. She needn't have said who she was. I remembered that in 1940 Sally had made her debut in Richmond, and I had taken her to a debutante party. I took her to a dinner and she was very popular and I did not see much of her because she was interrupted by other men all evening, and I had not seen her since.

"Sally was working at the Chalfonte, and she said that other young people were going to dinner, and wouldn't I like to come. We went in the back to the Tin House to join others enjoying cocktails. Mind you, I have not had anything to eat since 6 o'clock in the morning in Richmond.

"They said, 'Oh, we're going to Wildwood to a bar, come on along.' I am so hungry, but we go the Wildwood bar, and on the way back, thankfully, they decided spontaneously to stop at a seafood spot, and we had wonderful raw clams. My first dinner in Cape May, raw clams. I

ROW THE BOAT
Kitchen staff and friends float on the floodwaters that reach all the way from the ocean to the Chalfonte steps. The hotel's legendary bellhop, Henry Thatch, is pictured on the porch in white shirt and tie.
Satterfield family collection

remember them as delicious, but I was starving.

"I was Meenie's guest, and a week went by and a few more days. We were having a good time. I was enjoying Sally's company, and the magic of the Chalfonte, the exception being rousted by Theodore every morning, maneuvering over and around me and hoisting a tremendous pole to fly the flag over the cupola.

"One day my sister called from Richmond and said, 'When are you coming home. Aren't you overstaying your welcome?' Sally said she would take me to the train. She helped me with my bag onto the train, and was saying goodbye, and she said, 'You don't really want to go, do you?' And, I said, 'No I don't.' Sally said, 'Well, don't go.' She picked up my bag, and we left the train and went back to the Chalfonte. Meenie could not have been sweeter. I stayed a few more days and finally needed to return to Richmond to prepare for my music students.

"In Washington, DC when I transferred trains, I sent a telegram to the Chalfonte. In those days guests sent telegrams when they forgot something at the hotel. I wrote: 'Left behind... one heart... please send.' Two days later I received a big box, and wrapped in it, a heart – a heart made of soap.

"Sally and I continued to see each other, but we did not marry until 1949. It was wartime and Sally went off to England in the Red Cross. In the course of her service, Sally became great friends with Nancy Astor, wife of Lord Astor. Nancy came from Virginia and in typical Virginia fashion, mutual friends said you must look up Sally Jackson of Richmond. Sally was invited to Cliveden, the Astor estate for the weekend. There was a time when Nancy was called away after planning a weekend at Cliveden and she asked Sally to act as hostess for a houseful of notable guests. Sally possessed a lightning sense of humor. She had the ability to put any situation at ease, at Cliveden or the Chalfonte.

"Summer at the Chalfonte was very casual, very charming, was not formal in any way. There were cocktails before lunch, cocktails before dinner, cocktail parties in guest rooms. A fellow from Charlottesville who had never been there before asked why there weren't cocktails before breakfast. He arranged for an elegant breakfast on the beach. And he breaks out martinis and bourbon. Cocktails before breakfast!

"Very often there would be singing. We sang sentimental songs from the teens and 20s. A favorite of mine I learned from Sally's mother:

(609) 884-8934   301 Howard Street
Cape May, N.J. 08204

The Chalfonte Hotel offers:

All the charm, elegance, and atmosphere of the Victorian era

Excellent meals served family style with special Southern delicacies

A supervised children's dining room for youngsters under 7

Comfortable lodgings furnished with marble-top dressers and other Victoriana

Running water in rooms—bathrooms down the hall—some rooms with private baths are available

"Natural" air conditioning—courtesy of fresh sea breezes

A return to the peace of a former era—No TV or phones in the rooms (there is one "public" TV set available and two phones for guest use)

Restful surroundings—rocking chairs on porches and cozy balconies

"The Wine Cup", an Irish song. Singing was spontaneous. One summer, members of the Philadelphia Light Opera Company broke into song, in the dining room, on the porch. It was unusual and wonderful."

Sally Jackson Mead died May 7, 1989. Boots Mead, his two daughters, Jenny and Sally, and grandchildren continue to join the extended family for vacations and reunions.

(Boots got his name not because he was an equestrian, but because his mother hated his real name, Ernest and called him "Bootsie" after a friend of hers in Richmond. Sally had shortened his name to Boots, thinking it more fitting for a Virginia gentleman.)

When the Chalfonte season wrapped, Sally and her mother Lindsay spent time at the Mead family's property in Keswick, Virginia, foxhunting and showing horses. Boots rode, too, but says he was not as good as his wife.

Maria Carter Satterfield *Born 1925, Rich-*

SPORTS FIELD
This 1923 photo of the Chalfonte shows a University of Pennsylvania football practice on the lawn across from the hotel. Notes on the back of the photo read, in part, "Stayed at Chalfonte" and "Chalfonte porch: The Grandstand."
Donlin collection

A CHARM OF ITS OWN
Opposite: A Chalfonte brochure says there are amenities like "Natural air conditioning – courtesy of fresh sea breezes" and stresses "No TV or phones in the rooms."

mond, Virginia, wife of the late Calvin Satterfield III (1919-2005), son of Meenie and Calvin Jr "Our families knew each other in Richmond. My family vacationed in Cape May before I was married in 1949. I went to school with Sat's sister Nancy at St. Catherine's. My mother, Alice Blair Carter, and Sat's mother Meenie knew each other. Our families had been in World War I together, at camp together before our fathers, Robert Hill Carter and Calvin Satterfield Jr, went off to Europe. Then both our families' boys all went off to World War II about the same time. [Calvin Satterfield III received a Silver Star for gallantry crossing the Rhine River, and a bronze star for bravery.] After the war, there were wonderful debutante parties again in Richmond. At one of the debutante parties, Sat and I connected. We had a whirlwind time over two weeks – lunches, tea dances, dinner parties and the ball.

"Sat was quite a good equestrian. He was very athletic, and he courted me riding. I had a

grey horse that was a little too much for me. He rode my horse, and I rented one that was calmer. We rode the open fields and went fox hunting around Goochland.

"Sat spent all his boyhood summers in Cape May. When his mother and father owned the winter Chalfonte at Pinehurst, North Carolina, Sat, his brother Jimmy and sister Nancy began the school year in Pinehurst, transferred to Richmond in late winter months and finished up for one month in Cape May.

"Two of my daughters, Susan Neligan and Mary Minor Taylor, have purchased summer cottages across from the Chalfonte with back-yards that join so they can continue to partici-pate in the life of the old family hotel, and have meals there. My daughter Alice Tor rents cot-tages on Sewell Avenue. My son Calvin IV, his family [son Calvin V] visit in summer. The Chal-fonte relationship continues – now in a fourth, fifth, sixth generation with my 12 grandchildren

CRICKET AND MOM
This sort of iron single bed furnished most of the Chalfonte's rooms for decades. Here, Susie Satterfield's great-grandson, Cricket, is pictured with his mother, Sarah Lee Satterfield, in 1948.

JIMINY CRICKET
Opposite: Cricket Satterfield is among family members who have spent dozens of summers at the Chalfonte. He earned the name Jiminy Cricket from sounds he made as a newborn. He officially is named after his father, James Morris Satterfield.
Satterfield family collection

and one great grand-child. Remarkable, isn't it?

"My granddaughter Maria Neligan is work-ing at the Chalfonte this summer [2010] in res-ervations, a fifth generation to do so."

* * *

Cricket Satterfield was a few months old the first summer he spent at the Chalfonte. The year was 1947. His mother, Sarah Lee, tall at almost six feet, and leggy, possessed the looks and demeanor of a model and rejoiced in show-ing off her beautiful baby boy. He was named for his father, James Morris Satterfield, but has been called Cricket since birth. His maternal grandmother, Margaret Miller Blackburn, hov-ering over the newborn, wondered, 'What are the noises this child is making? Why that's my little Jiminy Cricket.' The name stuck. – there already were so many Jims in the family. When Cricket went off to prep school and his father thought it was time for him to be addressed as James, his mother sewed Cricket labels on all his

clothes, and the catchy name caught on again. He remains Cricket.

Cricket was pampered at the hotel by grandmother Meenie, Helen Dickerson, the head cook, and her daughter Dot Burton, also a cook.

Dot Burton "Cricket was an adorable baby. I cared for him a lot. I would take him, all dressed up, after work, and put him on the bar at Pete's [across the street from where the Acme is on Lafayette Street] and we would be drinking scotch and milk, and showing off Cricket. I am proud to say that even though he was the toast of Pete's bar, he grew up to be a fine polite and proper Virginia gentleman."

James Morris (Cricket) Satterfield *Born 1947, Richmond, Virginia; son of James Morris and Sarah Lee Satterfield, grandson of Meenie and Calvin Jr great-grandson of Susie Satterfield* "I summered at the hotel every year until I was about 14. Mother worked in the dining room and Dad went back and forth to Roanoke. I suffered an appendicitis attack on the boardwalk. A friend and I were eating chocolate licorice all day long, and I got a

SIT AWHILE
Above: Meenie Satterfield, her sister Rose, center, and her daughter-in-law Maria celebrate Meenie's birthday on the front porch.

MEENIE AND MARTHA
Opposite: The two Richmond ladies, both widowed at early ages, ran the hotel for almost 40 years. Martha Nash, right, was head housekeeper and Meenie Satterfield the owner.

THAT'S MY BOY
Right: Meenie and her beloved grandson, Cricket Satterfield. Cricket had a hiatus from the Chalfonte from age 12 until he he was discharged from the US Army. Then he committed to helping with the hotel.
Photographs by Judy Bartella

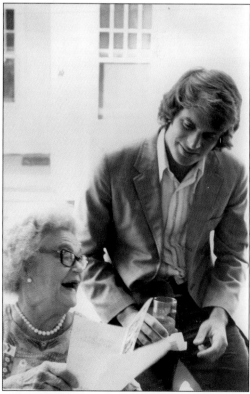

stabbing pain in my side. I made it back to the Chalfonte and Mother took me across the street to see Dr Tenenbaum. He gave me a shot and I went to bed, sick all night. The next day they took me to a surgeon in Wildwood, and surgery at Burdette. They called for a private plane from the Roanoke concrete company where my father worked. Mother said that was it – she was traumatized and scared, and she had no intention of returning to Cape May anytime soon.

"I had a hiatus from the hotel until I was about 21. Then I was out of the army during Vietnam when I was a medic, and I told Vovo, my grandmother ['Vovo' means 'grandmother' in Portuguese, and Meenie was born in Brazil] that I wanted to help her out. It was a renaissance for me, remembering my childhood, and now able to assist Vovo painting shutters, fixing screens, painting rooms, learning maintenance. 'Main-TAIN-ence', as we like to say. In the late

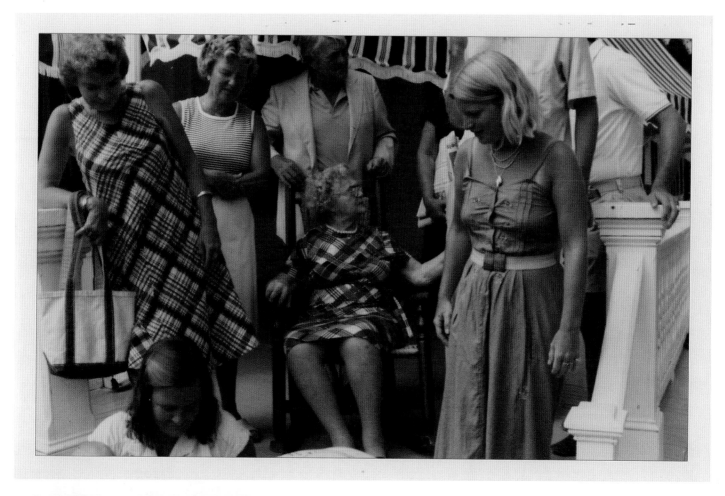

FAMILY REUNIONS
Opposite, top: Phoebe Peyton Hanson with her grandchildren in 1996. Elizabeth, Catherine, Mary Lynch are in the back; Sarah, Emily and Alison Ashby, twins Kevin and Michael in front.
Phoebe Peyton Hanson

Opposite, below: Calvin Satterfield IV, wife Louise and children, Lila and Calvin V.
Satterfield family collection

Above: Meenie Satterfield, center, with daughter Nancy, left, Maria Satterfield and husband Calvin III, their daughter Susan, right and daughter Alice, front.
Satterfield family collection

Left: Calvin Satterfield III and Phoebe Peyton Hanson, with Nancy Satterfield Davey, Susan Farris Jackson, and Cary Peyton, Phoebe's brother.
Phoebe Peyton Hanson

60s, early 70s, all rooms were the same pea green dating back to World War II. We went through a period where work weekend guests would decorate their rooms the way they wished. We had 100 rooms with 100 colors. I made a decision. We will have three colors: blue, and yellow in pastels and vanilla."

Cricket Satterfield helped his grandmother at the Chalfonte every summer until 1982, when it was time for the Satterfields to end their 70-year ownership. Meenie was approached by buyers who had ideas for condos, a dormitory for service workers, a parking lot and... demolition. Horrified that the oldest operating hotel in Cape May might be destroyed, two schoolteachers, Anne LeDuc and Judy Bartella, who had helped manage the hotel for more than a decade, took a leap of faith, got financing and purchased the sagging building. Theirs would be a miraculous mission and Cricket, along with some other Satterfields, stayed along for the adventure.

CHAPTER IV
Keeping Her In The Family

ANNE LeDuc has spent summers at the Chalfonte since she was two years old. She is 85 now and has loved the hotel for more than half of its 135 years. Her personality permeates the place. If it weren't for Anne and her deep affection for the old building and its lifestyle, there's a good chance it might have collapsed into a pile of gingerbread long ago. Or it might have suffered death by wrecking ball as the 1910 Christian Admiral Hotel did in 1996. Anne and fellow teacher Judy Bartella managed the hotel in the 1970s and bought the Chalfonte in 1982.

"The Chalfonte is one of the true loves of my life," says Anne. " More than a commercial hotel, more than a state of mind, it is about feeling, and people and recreating. The Chalfonte is a wonderfully supportive and caring community. It is my second home!"

Anne LeDuc, like the Chalfonte, defies easy description. She is intriguing in her devotion to preserving the aging building that has become a home away from home for a vast network of longtime friends and strangers who have become friends. Anne has a gift with people, making them comfortable by asking a question or so that opens the shell and begins a conversation that may end in a job at the Chalfonte and/or a lifetime friendship. The Chalfonte and Anne are about conversation and sharing, connecting, creating; always expanding the circle.

There are horse whisperers and dog whisperers. Anne is a people whisperer. Perhaps her talent comes from her background as a world-class athlete in field hockey and tennis and an athletic coach for decades. She runs her life and ran the Chalfonte with a team approach. As her friends and the staff at the Chalfonte will tell you, life with Anne at the helm of the Chalfonte was a sport of playing hard to save the hotel and its Virginia traditions and having a helluva good time while doing so.

She can be stern as a captain on the bridge in stormy seas, but she relaxes easily and shares her "big heart of pure gold," as staffers say. She possesses a humorous side and is always ready with a good one-liner or happy to entertain a crowd at the Tin House with a hilarious story. Her heart melts with every cat that crosses her

THE NATURAL
Ever since she was a child, Anne LeDuc excelled in athletics. Here she is pictured with the US field hockey team in 1956.
Anne LeDuc collection

HAPPY DAY
Previous page: Anne LeDuc during a wedding at the Chalfonte.
Chalfonte collection

path and orphans anywhere on the globe.

Anne is humble about her past as a star athlete who traveled the world playing Olympic quality field hockey (it was in the days before field hockey was an Olympic sport). She is modest about her ancestral pedigree, too, and only mentions it when pressed.

A continuous theme in the Chalfonte's life is its North-South connections. Civil War Colonel Henry Sawyer, a hero of the north, built the hotel, and Confederate daughter Susie Satterfield's family influenced the hotel as a southern

hostelry for more than 70 years. Anne LeDuc, a savior of the hotel beginning in the 1970s, has both northern and southern roots.

Her mother Bessie was the daughter of a lawyer from Lexington, West Virginia, Robert Catlett, whose grandmother was the daughter of US founding father Patrick Henry, famous for his "Give me liberty or give me death" speech. Anne treasures a Patrick Henry desk and some family letters. Bessie and Calvin Satterfield became friends when he was a student at the Virginia Military Institute in Lexington.

Anne can be stern as a captain on the bridge in stormy seas, but she relaxes easily and shares her "big heart of pure gold."

Bessie married attorney Louis LeDuc, whose great-grandfather was an early settler of Minnesota and a Union general in the Civil War. So Anne LeDuc had a foot in both north and south worlds. Her mother, a southern belle, first settled with her husband in Haddonfield and then Moorestown, New Jersey. She was a Latin teacher, but never got accustomed to living in New Jersey. She missed the southern way of life and returned to it every summer, joining with the Satterfields and other southern friends at the Chalfonte.

Anne's father is remembered with endearment by the older Chalfonte guests. He wore seersucker suits, and was impressive in his demeanour and pinz-nez. He was an intriguing conversationalist, a lovely man, and an outstanding trial lawyer. He was also the attorney for Victor Talking Machine, later known as RCA.

Anne enjoyed a storybook childhood. She attended Haddonfield Friends School, where she excelled in sports. "When I was five, I was the only girl on the baseball team," she says, matter-of-factly, "and I was probably better than all the boys." Anne was a precocious child. "Neddie Pennypacker and I were held back from first grade because we were so bad. I used my creative joy to cause havoc. Kindergarten didn't want to keep us, so they created a connecting

FAMILY ALBUM
This page, clockwise from top left: Anne LeDuc's mother, Bessie, lived for summers at the Chalfonte; Anne and her little brother Kit who became an artistic, athletic young man; Anne's father Louis LeDuc, a trial lawyer, enjoying a break at the Chalfonte; Anne with grandfather Robert Catlett, whose grandmother Celine was Founding Father Patrick Henry's daughter.

GIDDY-UP
Opposite: On a rented pony at Cape May's Convention Hall.
Anne LeDuc collection

class. Neddie and I were its only members."

In 1937, when Anne was in seventh grade, her family moved to Moorestown so she and her brother Kit would have the opportunity to go to Moorestown Friends School. Anne still lives in her childhood home, a 1924 white Colonial on two acres, featuring "Magic Mountain," a wooded hill. Anne, her brother and friends played field hockey, football, baseball and lacrosse on the lawn. The property was surrounded by an apple orchard, a barn and a path to nearby Strawbridge Lake. Anne has since donated half of the property to the city as a children's park.

Anne was a serious athlete in high school, earning a scholarship in tennis to Rollins College in Winter Park, Florida. She became weary

practicing tennis five hours a day and transferred her energies to field hockey. She earned a spot on the US Touring Team and traveled the world, playing in South Africa, Britain, Australia and the Fiji Islands.

She went on to coach athletics in Baltimore, Maryland and Montclair, New Jersey before settling into an extended coaching career at Quaker George School in Newtown, Pennsylvania. She coached swimming, lacrosse, basketball and field hockey from 1963 to 1993, when she retired to devote her energy full time to the Chalfonte.

It was at George School where she met fellow teacher, art instructor Judy Bartella, who first came to the Chalfonte in the summer of 1967 for recuperation after a trip to Tanzania, East Africa. She was quite ill on her return, and

"When I was five, I was the only girl on the baseball team," she says, matter-of-factly, "and I was probably better than all the boys."

remembers being nursed back to health with cook Helen's strained vegetable soup.

Judy grew up in Lexington, Kentucky and accepted the George School teaching job after graduating from Swarthmore College, Swarthmore, Pennsylvania.

Judy Bartella *Newtown, Pennsylvania:* "I totally fell in love with the building, its architecture and history. Then I met Mrs Satterfield and Mrs Nash and fell in love with the ladies and the Chalfonte way of life. I continued to visit the hotel in the 70s and began helping out. Mrs Satterfield had this great big reservation book and you needed to mark reservations in the book with itty-bitty numbers in pencil. We handwrote and mailed reservation confirmations. At the front desk Mrs Satterfield had a little cloth

LIFE OF THE PARTY
Above: Anne LeDuc frolics on the Cape May beach with Mac Rinehart.
Satterfield family collection

OLD FRIENDS
Left: Judy Bartella and her dog Sparky at Diddy's home in Washington, DC.
Judy Bartella collection

HOLIDAY PARTY
Opposite, top: Anne with friends Joan Stiles and Chickie Poisson.
Anne LeDuc collection

TIME OUT
Opposite, right: Anne's friend and Chalfonte partner, Judy Bartella, center, hosts a Magnolia Room breakfast with her sister Cathy Kriss, Nancy Dowlin and Judy's stepmother Brenda Bartella.
Judy Bartella collection

wallet with her monogram MMS on it, and that is where she kept the bills and checks and tied it with a little string. Cash was stored in a little tin box. I introduced a cash separator, completely transforming the front desk. That was my early contribution to management!

"In the 70s, Anne and I had a role in helping Mrs Satterfield manage the hotel. We developed a sense that we wanted to save the building and the way of life. For me, it was a mission. A mission to assure this hotel would be cared for. Of course our concern was for hospitality and the comfort of our guests. But I wanted this building to survive. I saw the fire at the Windsor, and it had a lasting effect on me, to see that wonderful historic building destroyed in flames.

"The Chalfonte is a monster that gobbles up all resources – financial, emotional and physical. I remember in the early years working into the night – painting the fire escape because the fire inspector was coming the next day.

"Anne and I developed work weekends, first with University of Pennsylvania students whose

professor John Milner, architect, gave historic lectures in Cape May. The U of P relationship followed naturally the work of preservationist Carolyn Pitts and the Penn architectural team she assembled to accomplish the lasting work of the measured pen and ink drawings of more than 60 Cape May historic structures in this National Historic Landmark city.

"Fate is responsible for the successful, two-decade University of Maryland architecture program. Professor David Fogle was critical of the hotel's condition and decided not to stay for dinner. I overheard him and later, chatting in the King Edward bar, we learned that we both grew up in Lexington, Kentucky. That fact developed a bond, and by the end of the lengthy conversation, Mr Fogle agreed he would like to help save the Chalfonte and initiate an architectural student work program for credit. The program began the next year in 1979 and ran until 2001.

"We had a policy that if we heard criticism we would attempt to address it, and turn it around. Ron and Jule Campbell, editors at *Fortune* and *Sports Illustrated* magazines, stayed at the Howard Street Cottage, and for reasons no one figured out, a dead fish turned up outside their door. They were insulted and ready to leave. Anne intervened and asked them to come out on the porch for a drink, and a conversation led them to stay on. They have been returning for almost 50 years.

"A favorite Chalfonte story is about the Chinese opera singer who had recently won a Pavarotti contest applying for a job. Because his English was so poor, we gave him a job to work on the roof. He was wonderful, chipping away the paint, and belting out opera in many languages. He caused quite a stir in the neighborhood as his songs floated from the rooftop. The second year his chipping deteriorated (though the singing was fine), so we needed to end the arrangement.

"I've learned the staff called me The Enforcer. In our earlier years, my job was to usher out the happy talking patrons from the King Edward Bar at closing and keep the volume down. Up stairs and down the long porches, windows were open – no air conditioning – and our guests were sleeping. It was a challenge.

"The Chalfonte enjoys good timing. It was time when Anne and I bought it from Mrs Satterfield; time for new energy and commitment and restoration. Cape May at the time was in a renaissance. Others wanted to buy it, but Mrs Satterfield was loyal to her family's hotel and

From The Archives

Excerpt from The Chalfonte Newsletter, 1982: "Old Hotel, Old Managers, New Owners."

As many of you know, we took on management of the hotel several years ago on an interim basis, hoping to stabilize the hotel and ensure its future. Now, thanks to the support of the Satterfields and all of you folks who have been, are and will be loyal Chalfonters, we have taken the next major step to buy the hotel. Our plan is to continue the Chalfonte as the type of hotel it has been for 106 years, to make structural improvements to maintain the long term existence of the Chalfonte as a building and to make the hotel an increasingly comfortable and pleasant place to stay. We thank you for your support and helpful criticisms in the past and look forward to many years of continuing to serve you, the Chalfonte and the community.

In order to facilitate and speed the structural stabilization phase of our program, we have applied for an urban development action grant (UDAG) to complete critical repairs to the building. With increased Federal budget cuts, we have our fingers crossed but are hopeful.

– Anne LeDuc & Judy Bartella

wanted to assure the buyers would not make it into a condo or a parking lot. We took out a bank loan (and Anne mortgaged her home) and the Satterfield family held the mortgage with an agreement they would receive discounted rates on rooms so they would come in family groups as they always had. We paid off the hotel in 10 years, but costs always escalated, and every season we needed to borrow money to open.

"Originally when we made the decision to buy it our lawyers said that we were purchasing it for the wrong reasons. Soon after, my father, at six-foot-five, visited. We proudly put him in room 40, the premiere corner suite, with the private bathtub – the petite private tub. He was aghast. 'Judy,' he said, 'buying this hotel is the worst decision you have ever made.'

"Now with the Mullock family purchasing the hotel, again the timing is good. It's in the hands of an extended family as it was with the Satterfields. And it's time for new energy and new renovations with air conditioning for the first time in 135 years and private baths."

The nearly $3 million the Mullock family paid enabled Anne and Judy to pay off the substantial debts they had accumulated in 24 of the 25 years they owned the hotel. The one year they made a profit, a friend, George Herzog, chastised Judy when she complained about the profit being only $176. He said, "A profit is a profit."

Judy says that she and Anne always poured their earnings back into the hotel for maintenance and upgrades. "We counted on friends and work weekenders to take up the slack. We never envisioned the hotel as a profit center. We were interested in preserving the building and the Chalfonte way of life. Relieved of the stress of increased borrowing and passing the hotel into loving competent hands, committed to ensuring the continuation of the Chalfonte and her traditions, were compensation enough for our years of labor and devotion."

Judy still teaches ceramics at George School and says she will stay until they take her out feet first. She has been head of the Art Department, is an accomplished potter and also paints.

But Judy combines her artistic side with an iron will and a desire for precision and order. Anne says that without Judy's sense of legal, financial and business matters, the two of them would not have succeeded in saving the Chalfonte. "She deserves much of the credit," says Anne. "Isn't it unusual that you can do business with your closest friend for over 30 years!"

Taking Care Of Safety... And Comfort

Excerpts from The Chalfonte Newsletter, 1982...

MORE COMFORT

Our hopes for new mattresses for the summer of 1981 were scrapped and the money was rechanneled into a smoke detection system for the hotel, which included battery operated smoke detectors in each room.

This winter we plan to purchase 30 mattresses for the rooms and plan one ALL NEW bathroom and upgrading of showers.

Also please pass the word along that the bathhouse now has both HOT and COLD running water for both the "Gulls" and "Buoys."

RESTORATION NEWS

There will be some surprises in store for you in the

FIRE ALARM
Cape May firemen rushed to the Chalfonte in 1987 to extinguish a minor blaze in the cupola. The cupola served as a special bedroom and the spot from which the big flag is raised and lowered.
Chalfonte collection

summer of 1982 if you were unable to visit us this past summer!

Thanks to a group of 30 University of Maryland students under the leadership of David Fogle, the lobby, reading room, writing room and King Edward Bar have been renovated.

The students put new ceilings in the lobby and writing room, both of which were desperately needed.

They also scraped, spackled and painted all the walls and color coordinated them to make the entire first floor common rooms of the hotel a continuous visual pleasure.

New curtains for the lobby and the newly recovered lobby furniture have given the entire area a new look.

The Essence Of Anne

NO ONE knows Anne LeDuc better than Judy Bartella. The two managed the Chalfonte for Meenie Satterfield for nine years from 1974 to 1982, then purchased and operated the hotel for 26 years. On Anne's 80th birthday, in 2005, there was a big party at the Tin House and Judy, in her words, shared the essence of Anne...

I HAVE known Anne LeDuc for most of my adult life and a good part of our friendship has been involved with the Chalfonte. I met Anne in 1967 when I first arrived at George School and Anne took me, the new teacher, under her wing. After I had a rough spring on a school work camp to Africa, Anne introduced me to the Chalfonte for a recuperative stay. Bringing me into the Chalfonte community as her friend immediately elevated my status and had Chalfonte staffers, as they typically do, going out of their way to be of service. Helen, our beloved cook and mother of Dot and Lucille, helped nurse me back to health, sending hot soup to the third floor to settle my tummy. Theodore, our beloved handyman and no spring chicken at that time, insisted on carrying my bags himself. I sensed I was in good hands.

Meeting Meenie Satterfield and Martha Nash, the two women who ran the hotel, was another high point. Both women had wit and charm and spent every summer day serving the Chalfonte and her guests. They were wonderful role models and great story-tellers, helping to connect generations of Chalfonte guests. They adored Anne, but it was not always the smoothest of relationships. Anne walked a thin line between being a rabble-rousing partygoer and the Chalfonte manager who tried to quiet the rabble-rousing partygoers! As anyone from that time can tell you, Anne and her friends ALWAYS

BIG SWEEP
Armed with a broom, Chalfonte owner Anne LeDuc surveys flood waters surrounding her hotel in September, 1985. Hurricane Gloria, flooded the dining room, but Anne and crew cleaned up in time for a wedding the next day.
Chalfonte collection

had a good time. Anne was always at the center of the fun, encouraging guests and staff to sing and put on skits in the annual talent show. This behavior would now be termed "community building," and is one of Anne's strongest skills.

One of my favorite Chalfonte memories is having early morning coffee with Meenie and Martha and Anne. We would meet to gossip and strategize about the day. Anne had brought an elderly Siamese cat to live in her bedroom on the third floor. So Meenie, Martha and I would be sitting and chatting and Anne would come down gruff and sometimes grumpy. We would greet her with a pleasant "Good morning!" and she would respond with a grunt or a "hummmft." But then the cat would round the corner and enter the room and immediately Anne's demeanor would change. Her face would brighten and the pitch of her voice would rise as she started cooing, "Here puddy, puddy. How's my little puddy this morning."

Perhaps one of Anne's greatest gifts is connecting people with one another. There are many families and individuals who have met and become fast friends with other families and individuals at the Chalfonte because of Anne's seemingly simple introductions. I am unable to ascertain if it is Anne's uncanny intuition about people and who would "fit" with whom, or her relentless passion for having people know one another in a warm and supportive context.

It is this passion for connecting people that drives Anne's unremitting love for the hotel. I have seen her exhausted and dog-tired, slumped in a chair in the lobby unable to move after a long and full Chalfonte weekend. A tourist wanders into the lobby and asks the desk clerk, "Is this the Chalfonte?" or "Do you serve dinner?" or "How much is a room?" Anne bounces off the couch to tell "The Chalfonte story" – or more importantly, to make a potential new guest feel welcome. For Anne, it is as natural as breathing. And for the Chalfonte, it has been the key to the hotel's continued existence.

A little known fact about Anne is that she has a computer for a brain. She has astounded me with her knowledge of the rooms and the

NEW OWNERS
Anne LeDuc and Judy Bartella in 1982 after purchasing the Chalfonte from the Satterfield family. Through its history, women have been primary operators of the hotel.
Chalfonte collection

The CHALFONTE

bedding configuration in each room. One year the city inspector asked me to do a schematic of which way each room door opened. Anne completed the task perfectly – from home! Much to the delight (or dismay) of the reservations staff over the years, Anne has been able to take a full hotel and rearrange the reservations (sometimes calling people to ask questions about the configuration of their party) so that we could accommodate one more couple. It is astonishing what that woman can keep in her head!

Anne is also known by friends and staff for her habit of losing, or should I more politely say, "misplacing", her keys. She has the worst key karma of anyone I have known. One of my proudest accomplishments early on in my Chalfonte career was to secure and have on hand at all times TWO additional sets of Anne's car keys. One was placed in the Chalfonte safe and one I kept at all times. Of course, these sets had to be replenished from time to time, as Anne lost her set and needed a replacement.

Over the years, she has lost a lot of things, but Anne is being honored today for something she saved. Over the years she has saved a lot of stuff, but her proudest save is in fact the Chalfonte. Many people have devoted huge amounts of time and energy and work and love to this institution, but none more than Anne. She has kept the hotel going despite huge odds against its survival

A few years into our Chalfonte business partnership, Anne and I did a workshop to evaluate whose talents lay where and perhaps fine-tune our hotel jobs. We were given 40 different values to put in order. For me it was easy. The first value on my list was "world at peace." Wasn't that true for everybody? What topped Anne's list was "loyalty". I was curious about that then, but now, as I reflect back on that, it is Anne's essence. It is the reason we have been best friends for nearly 40 years. It is the reason the Chalfonte is still going. Anne not only has loyalty, she inspires it. She inspired it in generations of students and has inspired it in generations of Chalfonte staff and guests.

THE PERFECT GIFT
Anne LeDuc holds up a shirt saying 'Hang in There Baby.' The shirt was given to Meenie Satterfield, left, for her 80th birthday. Her sister Rose is sitting to her left.
Photograph by Judy Bartella

The Chalfonte

"Anne is also known by friends and staff for her habit of losing, or should I more politely say, 'misplacing', her keys. She has the worst key karma of anyone I have known. One of my proudest accomplishments early on in my Chalfonte career was to secure and have on hand at all times TWO additional sets of Anne's car keys."

SEEING DOUBLE
Above: Judy Bartella, ceramic artist, in her signature studio apron, holding out the little clay critters for which she's known. The portrait on the wall was painted by fellow George School art teacher Pam Grumbach.

JUST ROCKING
The green rocking chairs on the Chalfonte's wrap-around porches are a beloved feature of the old hotel. Anne LeDuc and Judy Bartella take a moment in the rockers soon after buying the hotel in 1982.
Chalfonte collection

Anne LeDuc's 80th Birthday Tribute

By Pip Campbell, extracted from Anne LeDuc's 80th birthday scrap book, which was produced by Debra Donahue.

I WONDER IF when Anne was 10 years old and a guest with her family could she have possibly known that her summer vacations would turn out to be a lifetime commitment – that she would thrive on 70 summers of high-fat, high-cholesterol, oh-so-nurturing and oh-so wonderful southern food?

Any of us may look back over the history of the hotel and come to the same few conclusions. One is that Anne and Judy have made this wonderful place of timelessness work through shear tenacity, perseverance, cleverness and commitment. How remarkable that two women would take this challenge on in the 70s and manage not just to keep up with repairs but to actually improve and restore the buildings and to do it with no money. What better way for historic preservation students to learn about historic preservation than to help restore the hotel? What a great idea – work weekends that attract many people year after year – that attract people who want to contribute in whatever small way they can.

But – it really isn't the building. It is the values and beliefs that are woven into buildings in ways that make the two inseparable. What people hold dear are the traditions that take place in buildings.

And so it is with the Chalfonte. So maybe those folks on the carriage or the trolley rides or the walking tours find the building itself interesting, but what is important to most of us are the things that have happened at the hotel. Have other folks besides my friends had The World's Largest Urinal contests?... So how about the art shows, cabarets, musicians, movies, or other cultural events that we have enjoyed year after year.

In this show-me-the-money century, I find Anne's commitment to the hotel and to her community to be remarkable. That she has wanted to maintain some sense of tradition and to use her talents and her building to contribute to Cape May is unusual. So many others purport a same purpose while taking the money and running. So I put Anne on my list of incredible people who make a difference for her tenacity and perseverance, for taking on this great challenge and making it a personal commitment.

Above: John "Johno" Alexander. Opposite: Anne enters her 80th birthday celebration under a canopy of raised, festooned hockey sticks.

Photography by John Lynner Peterson

Carol Ann Baker and Anne LeDuc

Right: Kendal Stackhouse and Sondy Sonderskov

Architect John Milner being served

David Fogle and Linda Riccio

Chalfonte general manager Nancy Granick

John Court, Sarah Rohrbach, Nancy Wyatt, Sally Rohrbach

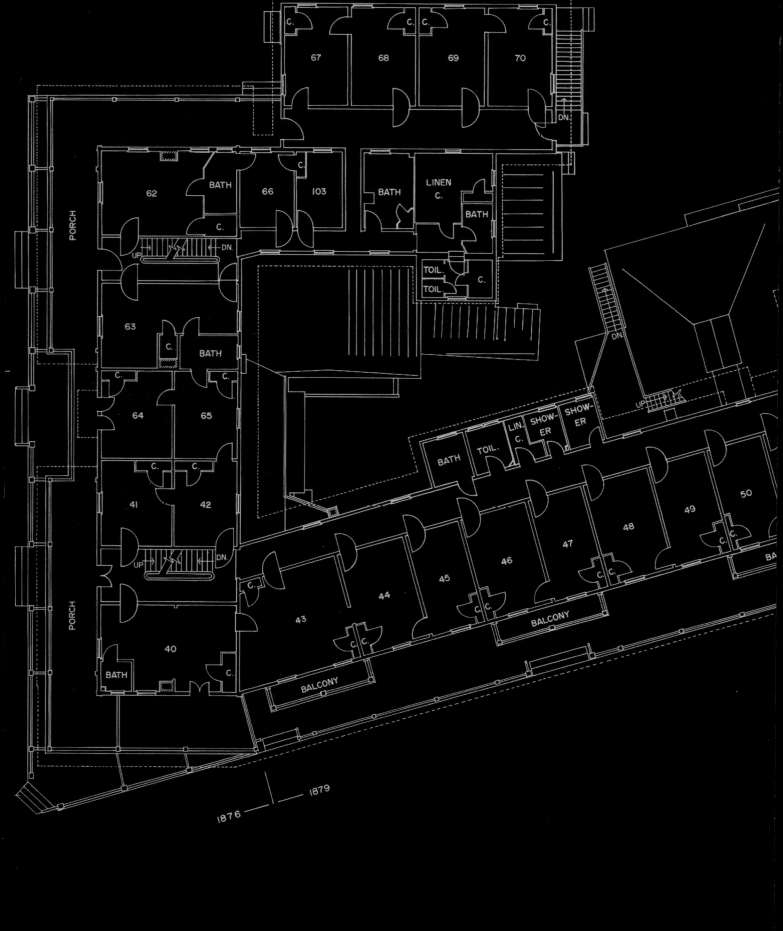

SECOND FLOOR PL.

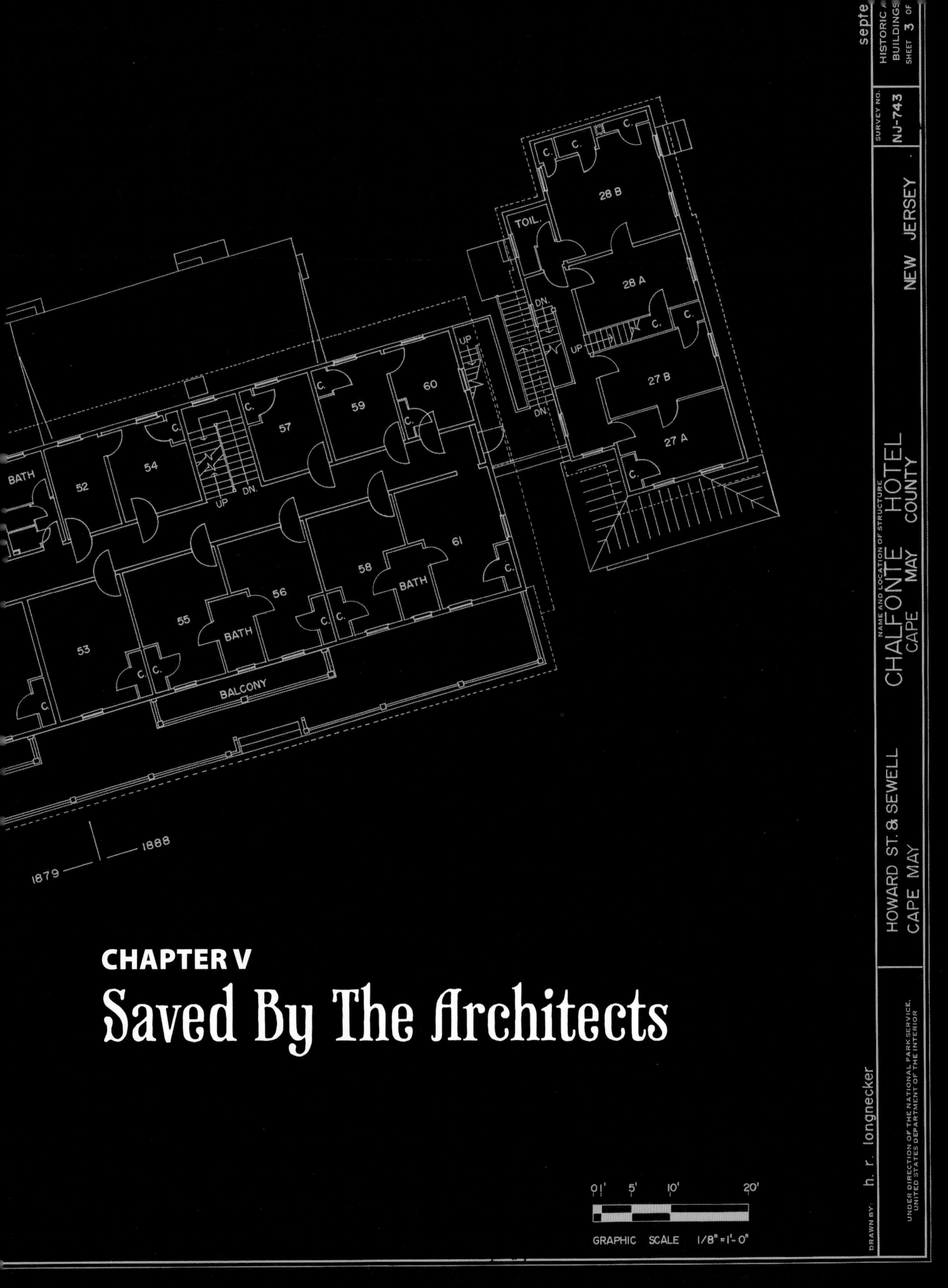

septe

SURVEY NO.
NJ-743

HISTORIC
BUILDINGS
SHEET 3 OF

C.
C.

28 B

TOIL.

28 A

DN.

UP

DN.

27 B

27 A

C.

C.
C.

UP

60

59

57

54

BATH

52

C.

C.

C.

UP
DN.

61

58

BATH

56

55

BATH

53

C. C.

C.

C. C.

C.

BALCONY

1888

1879

NAME AND LOCATION OF STRUCTURE

CHALFONTE HOTEL
CAPE MAY COUNTY

NEW JERSEY

HOWARD ST. & SEWELL
CAPE MAY

DRAWN BY: h. r. longnecker

UNDER DIRECTION OF THE NATIONAL PARK SERVICE,
UNITED STATES DEPARTMENT OF THE INTERIOR

CHAPTER V
Saved By The Architects

GRAPHIC   SCALE   1/8" = 1'- 0"

0 1'   5'   10'   20'

ARCHITECTURE professor David Fogle was appalled when he first visited the Chalfonte. He was in Cape May for a weekend with members of the Preservation Roundtable of Washington, DC. They rented an entire B&B on Jackson Street. As evening arrived, one of the group suggested they have dinner at the historic Chalfonte, famous for its downhome southern cooking.

Fogle, on entering the Chalfonte dining room, was shocked by its appearance. "It was dark and dreary and green paint, the color of split pea soup, was flaking off." Fogle was vocal about his disappointment. "I don't want to eat here. This place is too depressing."

A young woman approached him and introduced herself as Judy Bartella, manager. She apologized for Fogle's disappointment. She explained the entire hotel was painted pea green because that was the only color available during World War II, and afterwards the pea green was continued so all the rooms matched.

"I was mortified," says Fogle. "She had heard my every word." Fogle, a most charming man, apologized to Bartella. Fogle and friends decided not to have dinner at the hotel, but were fascinated by the architecture and looked around the building. Fogle and Bartella continued their conversation in the King Edward Bar later. They learned they were both from Lexington, Kentucky. The bonding began and before the night was over, the two were talking about how Fogle would help save the Chalfonte.

The year was 1979 and by the spring of 1980, Fogle, director of the University of Maryland graduate program in historic preservation, had created a work-study program involving 20 top architectural students. At the beginning of each season the students performed three weeks of preservation work in return for credits.

David Fogle AICP *Professor Emeritus of University of Maryland School Architecture, Planning & Preservation Annapolis, Maryland & Rehoboth Beach, Delaware* "Our first summer, the summer of 1980, there was skepticism. Would the program work? The Chalfonte managers were very dubious. The students received six credits for two legitimate architectural preservation

LACE AND GINGERBREAD
The Chalfonte is the oldest and most ornate hotel in the National Historic Landmark City of Cape May. The hotel opened to guests in 1876. The porches catch breezes from the Atlantic Ocean two blocks away.
Chalfonte collection

THE SAVIOR
Opposite: The late Carolyn Pitts is the woman who led the successful effort to draw, catalog and preserve Cape May's wonderful collection of 600 frame buildings from the Victorian era. She worked tirelessly, and behind the backs of local officials, to fight for Cape May National Historic Landmark status.
Perry Benson collection

INSIDE JOB
Previous page: Architectural rendering of the Chalfonte's interior by H. Reed Longnecker for the Historic American Buildings Survey, September, 1973.
Library of Congress

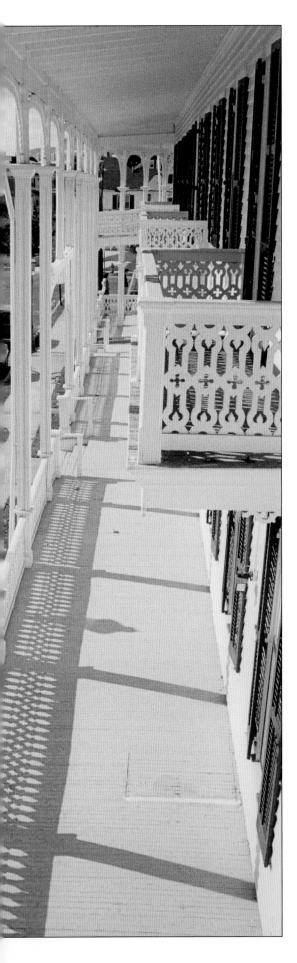

courses in two to three weeks. The students did hands-on restoration work and received free room and board. The students loved the program immediately. It was in the field, interesting work, in an authentic historic building and setting. Cape May recently had been named a National Historic Landmark for its collection of Victorian buildings. It was far more interesting than a textbook and traditional classroom setting. Soon the hotel management loved the program as well. Our first project: the dining room. We transformed the whole room. We got rid of that sick pea green paint and created new colors based on paint analysis of original ones.

"Our typical day: We had breakfast 8-8:30 and then planned the day's work. We worked hard from 9 to 1, had lunch at 1pm, and then free time to bicycle ride, go to the beach, look around town at other historic buildings. We got together for dinner with guest lecturers: For instance, architect Hugh McCauley, who supervised the scale drawings for the National Trust Historic American Building Survey. We had Preservation Roundtables. In 1984 there was a week-long conference on Historic Preservation

HAND DRAWING
In the early 1970s, University of Pennsylvania architecture students drew by hand, in pen and ink, measured drawings of all important Victorian structures in Cape May. Above, Perry Benson uses a pen as thin as a hair to replicate the Chalfonte's Howard Street façade. Benson's drawing is shown on the following page.

DOWN TIME
Opposite, top: Carolyn Pitts, left, and Perry Benson take a break from the drawing board.

MEASURED APPROACH
Opposite, below: Hugh McCauley at his drawing board at the Baronet. Carolyn Pitts selected McCauley as chief architect of the measured drawings for the Historic American Buildings Survey.
Perry Benson collection

centered at the hotel, bringing in experts from Philadelphia, Washington and elsewhere and dignitaries in the preservation field.

"Carolyn Pitts, the woman responsible for leading the city into National Landmark status, gave a trolley tour, among other presentations. Carolyn described in detail the buildings, the architects, the periods of history. She was impressive as she always was. Three couples restoring B&Bs participated: Tom and Sue Carroll who did such an outstanding job restoring the Mainstay B&B; Dane and Joan Wells, who likewise restored the Queen Victoria B&B; and Jay and Marianne Schatz, who preserved the Abbey. It was an exciting time in Cape May. The creativity, the commitment, it was the best of times in preservation in Cape May.

"I think the most effective teaching tool for preservation is field work. The students meet people who live in historic houses, and they learn how much those houses mean to the homeowners, how the homes affect their lives. The University of Maryland program ran from 1980 to 2000 – for 20 years and received national attention for its positive results.

CHAL

SOUTHWEST

K&E 19 1253 1-74 MC2059*

TION

0 6" 2'   5'   10'

GRAPHIC SCALE   1/4"=1'-0"

DRAWN BY: PERRY BENSON

UNDER DIRECTION OF THE NATIONAL PARK SERVICE,
UNITED STATES DEPARTMENT OF THE INTERIOR

HOWARD ST. & SEWELL
CAPE MAY

NAME AND LOCATION OF STRUCTURE
CHALFONTE HOTEL
CAPE MAY COUNTY

NEW JERSEY

SURVEY NO.
NJ-743

JULY 1974

HISTORIC AMERICAN
BUILDINGS SURVEY
SHEET 5 OF 5 SHEETS

LIBRARY OF CONGRESS
INDEX NUMBER

LC-USZAI-1539

LANDMARK MOMENT
In 1976, John Milner, professor of architecture at the University of Pennsylvania, held student workshops at the Chalfonte. That year, staff celebrated the hotel's 100th anniversary... for the third year in a row. They had previously, and mistakenly, held 100th anniversary parties in 1974 and 1975, during which time there was confusion about the year that Sawyer had built the hotel. Chalfonte collection

BACK ALLEY
Above: A lot of Chalfonte life has happened here. It's where the peas and corn are shucked; where the laundry is done. It's where the staff takes breaks and in the evening, where songs are sung.

SIMPLY ELEGANT
Right: The Chalfonte is one the most photographed buildings on the Eastern Seaboard. This photo shows details of its eclectic Victorian architecture.

NATURAL AIR
Opposite: For 133 years, the Chalfonte had no air conditioning: "Natural sea air," the brochures said. Banks of windows on shaded porches and transoms above bedroom doors allowed ventilation. Air conditioning was added in 2008 when the Mullock family bought the hotel.
Library of Congress

"Each year we focused on a project. The 1868 Annex, the building to the rear of the Chalfonte, was a major project. Students redid the lattice at the Tin House, and planted roses there. We were going to tear down the Tin House, the small pre-fabricated building to the rear of the hotel. Then we learned it was a sacred place, that it was where in Prohibition they stored the illegal alcohol and in later years, scene of many special events, parties and weddings. One year a student was committed to cleaning out all of the fireplaces. He did an outstanding job removing about 10 coats of paint from the mantel in the King Edward Bar, exposing the original walnut."

Fogle returned to the Chalfonte for a visit in May, 2010, catching the Cape May-Lewes Ferry from his Rehoboth Beach summer home. His affection for the hotel remains infectious.

"The Chalfonte was not always white. It has been since the 1890s, but before that it was sand colored with chocolate brown and yellow. We found the colors under layers of white. And the gingerbread! In our student projects we took

ROOFTOP SURVEY
The massive red roof has been a worry for more than a century. It requires constant maintenance due to its age, the many additions to the hotel and sea weather wear and tear.
Chalfonte collection

STUDY IN SHADOWS
Opposite, and next page: Architects and artists love the Chalfonte for how the sea light plays off its pillars and lace, creating different sets of shadows.
Library of Congress

out the rotting, unstable pieces and traced the pattern. We had a big power saw set up on the porch and cut the new gingerbread and inserted the pieces as you see here. The gingerbread replacing was one of the first projects every summer. The window above the Solarium – we found that covered with plywood. We carefully removed the plywood and found that the gingerbread was painted the original color of the hotel. The glass was painted too. We were able to expose the gingerbread and paint it white, but we could not save the old glass. We replaced the glass. On the other side of the Solarium there is an identical window, still covered with plywood. It would be good to restore this as well, but there are a lot of wires to be moved.

"Have you seen the antique urinal? I came upon some workmen considering removing this very large pissoir. I said, 'No no, this must stay. This is an important historic artifact.' And we enclosed it so it remains useful. (See page 218.)

"The Secret Garden, the space was not used. It was not attractive. One of the students took

the area on as a project and created this garden – now an oasis of green and color, especially appealing and cool in the heat of summer outside the kitchen, and lovely to peer into from the screen doors, lobby and dining room.

"Nostalgia has a lot to do with the Chalfonte's success – the fact that it not only is old, but it has an authentic persona and not only looks that way, but feels that way and has an emotion about it. The rockers on the porch give a continuity from one season to the next, one generation to the next, of friend to friend just sitting there talking and remembering and dreaming of what's next. And, when the old-timers go, they are remembered with small brass plaques on the backs of the rockers.

"Food has had a lot to do with the success of the Chalfonte. An authentic menu of old-fashioned southern country cooking like our grandmothers may have served. Identity is linked with a place, and preservation keeps those places intact, provides that identity, and makes people feel like they're somebody in that particular time zone.

"Originally the dining room walls were a sandy color, and the wainscot was the same chocolate brown as the exterior trim, and the ornamental plasters were red. We restored the chandelier by making little molds from the original and filling the molds with plaster that hardened, and we attached them to complete the design. I'll show you a secret. Look there. You will see that the mold isn't finished; that there is just stippling on the ceiling. I was helping put the finishing touches around the chandelier. The dining room was about to open with guests waiting at the door. Someone said, 'Move that ladder now,' and we took the ladder and made a fast exit and that project was never completed.

"I see where they've been working on the dining room floor. The whole floor on that end leaned down. It so leaned to an angle that the furniture tipped to that corner. The Sewell Avenue wing was added on in the 1890s, and its underpinnings were never right in the first place. Over the years, the earth shifts, and flood waters invade, and the wood finds its own level."

Hugh McCauley *Architect, Bryn Mawr, Pennsylvania, and Cape May* "The first time I saw the Chalfonte was in the late 60s. I had been haunting Cape May, coming down with friends at the University of Pennsylvania when nobody was in town, and it was quiet and we'd cruise around and look at houses and take photographs. We

From The Archives

▪ Preservation Awards, given by the New Jersey Department of Environmental Protection:

As the Chalfonte Hotel celebrates her 125th Anniversary this year, the owners can be proud of successfully preserving not only the fabric of this historic hotel, but also the experience of staying in a 19th century seaside hotel. The Chalfonte possesses integrity of design, traditions, culture and ambiance, providing a unique guest experience, while meeting the demands imposed by evolving customer needs and increased competition.

Such success was due in part to the help of the University of Maryland (UMD) School of Architecture's annual Preservation Program, and the hotel's ongoing Volunteer Work Weekends. Since 1980, UMD students and faculty have been participating in a three-week, hands-on summer preservation course at the Chalfonte. The resulting body of archival materials, field drawings, and restorative architectural projects has benefited hotel staff, guests, and the community-at-large.

In addition to the technical expertise afforded by the UMD program, the demands of seasonal maintenance required additional resources. So in 1982, based on the suggestion of several regular guests, the owners conceived the Volunteer Work Weekend, where guests receive accommodation in return for ten hours of maintenance work around the hotel. The popularity of the program grew quickly, such that the hotel now runs nine such weekends.

It is the commitment of the owners and participants in these two innovative programs that allow a 19th century hotel to carry on into the 21st century with a secure future.

had been looking at the Physick house. Tragic. Broken windows, leaky roof, shutters hanging. We looked at the row of houses on Congress Street, the early Victorian stock. And then the Chalfonte, a huge wedding cake of a thing, all dressed up, amazing; all white and sparkling, and old, very old. The location a surprise, set back from the beach the way it is.

"My involvement with the Chalfonte came with my involvement in the landmarking of the town. A Penn faculty member giving a party invited me. The party was going on, and this woman, she is a very large woman, came up to me, grabbed me by the collar and started lecturing me about supporting the preservation of the Physick house. She took me in a back room, and said, 'Now you are going to work for me.' This woman, larger than life, was Carolyn Pitts."

In 1970, Carolyn Pitts managed, without officials knowing about it, to get the city of Cape May listed as a National Historic Landmark. Three years later she was leading a team detailing 60 architecturally important buildings on paper. All were University of Pennsylvania educated. Called Operation Gingerbread, the team set up shop in the Baronet, a sea-whipped 1870s cottage on Beach Avenue.

Their mission: to measure precisely and draw exactly all the floor plans and architectural details of all the buildings with radiograph pens, some points thin as a single hair. The team

FIXING THE LACE
Above: Sea winds and sea salt take their toll on the hotel's ornate woodwork. Student restoration carpenters make repairs and replacements.
Chalfonte collection

FACELIFT
University of Pennsylvania work weekenders repair steps at the corner of Howard Street and Sewell Avenue. It is this corner of the Chalfonte that is most photographed.
Chalfonte collection

worked in 1973, 74 and 77. Hugh McCauley was chief architect. Participants were architects Perry Benson and H. Reed Longnecker, student architects Marianna Thomas, Jay Bargmann and Gardener Cadwalader, historian and chief draftsman Susan Stein, architectural interns Thomas Ewing and Dan Goodenow, draftsman-surveyor Daniel McCoubrey and Trina

Vaux, who was in charge of handbook preparation. The team needed expert people skills to coax their way in, over and under the historic structures to measure, analyze, photograph and sketch for their drawings. Some locals welcomed them with tea and cake. Others thought the project silly or government intervention and told them to beat it and get out of town. The architects talked the fire department into lending its large hook and ladder truck to climb the roofs of Congress Hall and the Chalfonte.

Cathy McConnon *Former Chalfonte desk clerk, Philadelphia, Pennsylvania* "I was packing up at the end of the season, preparing to leave for my winter Kelly Girl job in Coconut Grove, Florida. I had met some of the Penn students who had set up their drawing rooms at the Baronet. They asked if I would be secretary to the project.

"I took the job for two months and went over to the Baronet and worked every day. Perry Benson was putting his pen to the Chalfonte. When he was drawing, he would call me back at the hotel and say, 'The hall, the ocean side, will you check and see which way those doors swing open?' It was interesting and a good time working for the architects. The two months were up and it was time for me to head down to Florida, and Carolyn Pitts said, 'I'm out of money. I have no funds to pay you.' Perry Benson went out and bought 12 beautiful lobsters, and he hosted a lobster feast that night at the Baronet in my honor. The memory of it is priceless."

It was Perry Benson whose hand, in pen and ink, rendered the measured drawings of the Chalfonte for the Historic American Buildings survey, known as HABS. Drawing the Chalfonte was a challenge with its dozens of windows, shutters and long gingerbread verandas built in different decades. Its American Bracketed Villa style allows for extending the living space to the porches and balconies, bringing the outside seashore smells, sounds and breezes under roof which is an enduring charm of it.

On a visit to the Chalfonte in September 2010, Perry Benson remembered the way it was.

Perry Benson *Architect, Philadelphia* "We drew on velum, a cotton fiber, in pencil, and edited as we went along, the drawings getting dirtier as we went. The velum in the heat and humidity of the old Baronet on the ocean could expand by one fourth of an inch. You can imagine the frustration. We finished in ink on mylar. It was a painstaking effort. We were here in Cape May in 1973, 74, 77. Mrs. Satterfield was here at the time, and she loved the fact that the Chalfonte was being permanently preserved in the National Archives. I was invited to sleep in the cupola. It was considered an honor to do so. Mrs Satterfield sent me letters thanking me for copies of the drawings I sent her.

"We got on the porches and roofs, analyzed the balustrades – some were incorrect. Our job was to record the building not as one thought it should be, but as it actually was. There was a whole lot of freehand sketching before the measured drawings were committed to mylar.

"It was a time when there was a lot of worry about the historic buildings – the Chalfonte, the Macomber, the Windsor,. Would they survive? There were interesting characters in town then: the theatrical mayor Bruce Minnix, the radio preacher Reverend Carl McIntire, who was broadcasting from the high seas off Cape May.

"The Chalfonte then looked as if it were waiting for maintenance. I remember all-around maintenance man Theodore working at the coal-fired hot water heater. The hotel seemed more a curiosity and anachronistic than now – grand and undulating over the landscape."

"Many people come to Cape May without ever seeing it," wrote Jim Quinn in a 1976 *Philadelphia* magazine story. "They concentrate on the big hotels, like Congress Hall and the Chalfonte. Both are architect-less. The Chalfonte started as a medium-size boarding house, run

ORIGINAL AND BEST
Top: A student restores walls in the hotel lobby. Below: Professor David Fogle's team recreates moldings and paints original colors in the dining room.
U of MD School of Architecture, Planning and Preservation

by Colonel Henry Sawyer, a Civil War prisoner of war... Sawyer's boarding house prospered and kept it growing, adding rooms and lacey jigsaw filigree in careless profusion."

Quinn quoted Hugh McCauley: "The builder of this place was not an engineer and not a perfectionist, either. He stuck on things as they fit, and builders who came after him stuck on more as they fit. The first building went up in 1876,

Excerpt from *Town and Country* magazine, June 1980, by Dennis Lundt.

One of the most beloved survivors of the Belle Epoch is the huge old Chalfonte Hotel, whose funky charm each year brings back such loyal local guests as Mrs Gerald Montaigne of Kennett Square, Pennsylvania, wife of Pierre du Pont's private secretary and Duff Merrick from Barbados and Essex, Connecticut. Despite the threadbare rugs, sagging beds and verandas, and communal bathroom facilities, the Chalfonte's world-traveled guests overlook the many eccentricities of this grande dame and applaud her passé allure.

Mrs Mary Satterfield, the hotel's octogenarian owner, whose family bought the property in 1911, recalls how she motored north with her family each year "each of the children sitting on a large keg of bourbon." Well known for her quick wit and super southern charm, Meenie, as she is known to hundreds of admirers, reigns daily, June through Labor day, at Cape May's most outrageous, zaniest landmark.

"We're so old-fashioned and funny. I can't imagine why anyone comes here. We don't even have air conditioning or television," Mrs Satterfield warns guests. Many do threaten to check out the minute they see their Salvation Army-style rooms. But, more than likely, they stay on and on. "We don't have the comforts I'd want on vacation. But we're friendly and the food is good."

Still serving the same menu drawn up by her mother-in-law (Susie Satterfield) – fried chicken on Wednesday, country ham on Thursday, spoon bread every morning, hot rolls every night – the Chalfonte owner, her children and grandchildren concern themselves nowadays with the future of the hotel. Managed by Anne LeDuc and Judy Bartella, teachers at George School, the venerable property with its green and white awnings, is long on tradition and hominess, and is not only an architectural, but a social landmark.

the last addition in 1900. There were not many square corners on the building to begin with, and there are none at all now.

"Wood that's been exposed to sea air absorbs so much water that it almost turns to rubber in time. The structure still has vibrancy, but it sags and bends and dips to conform to the ground around it. Perry Benson did the drawing – first in pencil so he could get in all the details and mea-

TAKING A TOUR
Top: Professor David Fogle admires a day's work in preservation. Below: Student tour at the Emlen Physick Estate conducted by the Mid-Atlantic Center for the Arts.
U of MD School of Architecture, Planning and Preservation

surements exact – then he went over the whole thing again in radiograph, using the smallest point, .00000001 millimeter. The drawing was reproduced by the National Historical Building Survey as a recruiting poster. They made about 500 of them and stuck them up on walls at schools of architecture all across the country. They had to make 500 more because the drawing is so good the first batch got ripped off – and wound up on studio walls."

Perry Benson remembers, "There was a lot of national publicity generated by Carolyn Pitts and Operation Gingerbread. *Town and Country* magazine came to town to define society here and they had never encountered a culture like it. Mrs. Satterfield and the Chalfonte received prominent mention."

John Milner, *FAIA Professor, Graduate School of Design University of Pennsylvania, Principal John Milner & Associates, Chadds Ford, Pennsylvania* "The Chalfonte is a wonderful building. It has a spirit of its own. The best description of it came from Gary Gredell, structural engineer. We were talking about the condition of the building and how it settled here and there, and he said, 'Well, the building has just relaxed.' And that's exactly what it has done. It sits on sand and the foundations rise and fall with the water level and the shifting ground. The building has been able to react to that movement over the years. The building, because it is a frame structure, is much better able to react to changes. It has its own challenges, demanding very intensive maintenance, but it rolls with the punches and has for many years. It has received a lot of tender loving care, and if the TLC continues, the Chalfonte will continue to be itself for years to come.

"My wife Wynne and my association with the Chalfonte has been over a long period of time. I consulted with Anne LeDuc and Judy Bartella, owners, over specific architectural and structural issues. I really fell in love with the place. In the 1980s, teaching at the University of Pennsylvania graduate school of design, looking for hands-on projects for students on historic buildings, we scraped and painted porches and performed some carpenter work.

"Anne and Judy, always interested in adding cultural activities to generate interest at the hotel, learned I had attended wine school and that my wife and I gave small wine tasting events. We started a wine tasting program on Saturday afternoons. I bought the wines for the hotel and developed a list for the dining room. It

CHALFONTE CLASSROOM Top: Architect Brian McCarthy and wife Rula work on the King Edward Bar. Below: University of Maryland students repairing and painting porches and rockers. U of MD School of Architecture, Planning and Preservation

was a lot of fun.

"One of my most humorous experiences spun off the wine list. The Savoy Opera Company was performing at dinner. They came early and saw the wine list I had prepared. To amuse themselves, they started singing the wine list. They saw the wine notes and they sang the wine notes. One of them said to me, 'And what is it you do at the hotel?'

From The Archives

▨ Excerpt from the Chalfonte Newsletter, Spring, 1998: "About Restoration."

On November 18th of last year, John Milner, our architect for all of these years along with carpenter Ed Hallman, roofer Bill Clark, owners Judy Bartella and Anne LeDuc and maintenance manager Jim Abrams met to discuss major and minor architectural issues.

Some of the projects are underway or completed, including a new roof over the kitchen, refinishing the dining room floor and porch repair.

No discussion of the hotel's preservation and restoration would be complete without the University of Maryland's Architecture program, now in its 19th year.

The program is unique. Students receive academic credit and hands-on preservation instruction on a historic landmark.

Led by instructors David Fogle and Mike Arnold, the students studied handicapped accessibility, replaced porch columns and balustrades and completed many architectural drawings, with many new plans for spring.

▨ Excerpt from the Chalfonte Newsletter, Spring, 1996…

Friends of the Chalfonte
Cordially Invite You To the
Second Annual RAISE THE ROOF
Saturday, September 21 at 6:30pm
Attire: Chalfonte Black Tie

Because of the extensive roof restoration necessary and the underlying costs, the Friends of the Chalfonte gathered together in 1995 to help raise the much needed and much appreciated funds.

Last year's first annual Raise the Roof Gala helped immensely in the preservation of the roof over the front left porch. This year our aim is to continue these major efforts on the roofs over the kitchen and the right front porch.

Join us for a fantastic night of dancing to the seven piece swing band Big Night Out, a wonderful dinner and good company.

"I said, 'I write the wine list.'

"One summer I was wine steward on the weekends. I am serving wine to an architect from Princeton. He kept looking at me quizzically. I said, 'Bill, it's John Milner.'

"'Yes,' he said, 'I know. My God, John, what happened?'

"He thought I had lost my practice and was waiting on tables at the Chalfonte!"

LEADING THE WAY
Top: Professor David Fogle, Mike Fish and Carolyn Pitts discuss a restoration project. Below: Students cleaned, repaired and refurbished the hotel's original fireplaces.
U of MD School of Architecture, Planning and Preservation

Major Exposure For The Chalfonte

AN EXAMPLE of the national publicity generated by the University of Maryland work-study project came in the November, 1981 issue of *National Geographic*. A photograph of students restoring gingerbread taken by Michael S. Tamashita was spread over two pages (a student standing behind him shot this photograph, right).

Writer Jim Hartz, a former co-host of the *Today* show with Barbara Walters, ended his *National Geographic* story, titled "New Jersey a State of Surprise", by focusing on Cape May and the Chalfonte...

"Cape May received a three-million-dollar-urban renewal grant to stay old," a local scholar of New Jersey's past and present told me. One of the nation's oldest summer resorts, renowned years ago as the watering place of Presidents – Buchanan, Pierce, Harrison, Grant – Cape May is today a Victorian architectural gem. More than 600 structures from the last century survive.

The well-kept, turreted filigreed buildings grace winding, shaded streets. Hundreds of thousands of vacationers go there every summer to be transported back to a simpler, less hurried time. I stayed at the Chalfonte Hotel, a three-story, hundred-room structure built in 1876. Things haven't changed much since: no elevators, no air conditioning, no room phones, and the 'facilities' down the hall. It's still a grand old place and has the most wonderful cook in the world. Helen Dickerson, 70, has been cooking three meals a day for a hotel full of guests for 45 years. "I've never used any recipes," she said, stirring up homemade mayonnaise. "I just quit when it looks good."

Her specialties are prime ribs, kidney stew, southern-fried chicken, and spoon bread. She gets up before dawn every morning and does all the shopping. That's New Jersey hustle.

One evening, after the sun went down, I sat in a rocking chair on the hotel's wide veranda, watching strollers along Howard Street caught in the flickering reflections of gaslights in the center of town. Hotel manager Judy Bartella came out and asked if I was bored.

"We have an old television somewhere," she said. "I'll get it if you need a fix."

I declined the offer, preferring instead to while the evening away, silently wondering how I could have missed so many things in New Jersey in all those years. I lived so close. And, too, feeling a little sorry for all those people who never get off the road and see one of our most historic, productive and elegant states.

CHAPTER VI
Weekend Warriors

AY 7, 2010: It's one of those magical May mornings when the sea takes hold of the island. From the Chalfonte porch, you can feel, see and hear it. It's a special day all around. In the Magnolia Room, Henry Sawyer IV, the great-grandson and namesake of the Chalfonte's founder, is having breakfast with his wife and two daughters. Hal, as he likes to be called, is not here on vacation. He and his family are preparing for a work weekend at the hotel that his great-grandfather built. His daughters, Zoe and Arden, are fifth generation Sawyers to stay and work at the Chalfonte.

Hal and his wife Leila tell how they rode horseback on the Gettysburg, Pennsylvania Civil War battlefield to get a sense of the cavalry in which Henry Sawyer fought. They took

TEAMWORK
Above: The more hands the merrier the work as student volunteers scrape layers of paint from the Sewell Avenue porch railings.
Photo by Judy Bartella

WORK WEEKENDS
Opposite: Since the 1980s, volunteers have joined in preserving this special place. Pictured is the alley, with the Chalfonte cupola in the background.
Chalfonte collection

GOLDEN OLDIE
Previous page: Thanks to regular maintenance by the staff and enthusiastic volunteers, the 135-year-old Chalfonte is aging well.
Photo by Aleksey Moryakov

a trip to Brandy Station, in the beautiful rolling hills of Virginia, where Hal Sawyer's great-grandfather fought and was left for dead in the bloodiest cavalry battle in the war. Hal says the landscape remains untouched by development. One can hardly imagine the carnage that happened there.

Hal is the custodian of his great-grandfather's saber. "Have you ever seen that Camp Stoneman picture of him and his buddies? They look like tough hombres to me. I think I would stay on the other side of the street." (See pages 10-11.)

Hal shares more than a name with his great-grandfather. He is a carpenter as well. He restores historic buildings, mostly in the Germantown area of Philadelphia. For this Chalfonte work weekend he drove to Cape May in his carpenter's car, a vintage Volvo his daughter painted in colorful graffiti style. The back was packed with carpenter tools. Among Hal's jobs was to restore a fence where the roses grow by the Tin House. His wife and daughters chipped

paint from the front porch floor.

After lunch, Hal sat on an older wicker chair in the sun-drenched alley and reminisced about his great-grandfather. He talked in simple terms about his achievements on the battlefield, that he was a strong man to survive the life-threatening conditions inside Libby Prison. Ultimately he was saved from a Confederate firing squad and released because Abraham Lincoln had a personal recollection of meeting him early in the war, when Sawyer was among the first Union volunteers to guard Washington.

Hal Sawyer *Philadelphia* "It wasn't until Anne LeDuc bought the hotel that my family visited. She invited my father [Henry Sawyer III, a prominent Philadelphia lawyer] down and my brother Jonathan and me. I was in my late teens. My father never felt any real connection with the hotel. He did not spend a lot of time in Cape May. He would come to visit his grandmother, Mary McKissick Sawyer, a school teacher. She was Colonel Sawyer's second wife. My father never knew his father, Henry Sawyer II, born in 1890, who died before my father was born. Mary McKissick Sawyer passed on to my family the saber and photograph of Camp Stoneman.

"This building Henry Sawyer built was not meant to be permanent. It's being held together with lacquer and paint. The builders could never

GRANDE DAME MAKEUP
Left: Work weekender Linda Clauson paints a new face on the old hotel during a student preservation workshop.
Above: This room is losing its old plaster in preparation for new walls and paint.
Opposite: It's a tough job preparing for a new coat of paint on the porch. Pictured is Debra Fein, work weekender.
Chalfonte collection

have imagined, at 133 years in age, air-conditioning and new bathrooms would be added to this simple structure."

In the early 1980s, inventive co-owners Anne LeDuc and Judy Bartella created the volunteer work weekends. Guests receive room and board in exchange for 10 hours of work – such as painting, landscaping, installing awnings and repairing furniture. About 1,400 people, mostly repeat guests, have volunteered over the years.

Jim Abrams probably knows every nook and cranny of the Chalfonte better than anyone. He started in maintenance at the hotel in 1986. Much of his work was behind the scenes. In

LIFE IS GOOD For some Chalfonte devotees, the porch and the rockers are all they need. Photograph by John Lynner Peterson

Old Lady You Have To Love

Excerpt from "The Chalfonte Hotel Celebrates 130 Years", by Susan Tischler, published July, 2006 on Capemay.com...

You know a grande dame never compromises her standards. The times may have changed, but this lady still preserves a genteel life void of distractions. The Chalfonte offers guests, staff and visitors a chance to go back to a simpler time and she stands proud of the fact that the rooms have no air conditioning, no television, no telephone service, no Jacuzzi. What she does offer is the best in southern hospitality – good food, a chance to stay a spell and rock on the spacious wrap-around porch and a chance to learn the fine art of conversation.

Folks like "Mac" MacDonald haven't missed a year yet. Mac is from Freehold, New Jersey, holds a PhD in electrical engineering and tends to work on Lady Chalfonte's plumbing when he comes to town. The two are intimately acquainted that way. Mac even looks like a disgruntled lover when we chat with him one rainy Saturday afternoon.

Oh? She's a little needy, is she? Our question is, why do you keep coming back? He owned a Victorian house once and became so preoccupied with renovating it, he eventually sold it. Work Weekends at the Chalfonte allow him the pleasure of working on an old house and the satisfaction of knowing he can walk away from it. But he doesn't seem to walk away for very long. There are eight, sometimes nine, Work Weekends a year. Mac usually attends six or more of them….

Betty Merchak is equally smitten. This is her 29th time – her 16th year coming to

Work Weekends and she has kept a diary of every room she has stayed in, chronicling the work which was done to each room. "I started coming here in the 80s with my girlfriends," she says. She kept coming back when the girlfriends found other ways to spend their weekends and when she married her husband John, he joined her and now, they come to the Chalfonte.

"I love meeting old friends (who are also long-time participants) and it's such a feeling of accomplishment to know that I'm helping to keep the Chalfonte going. The first time I came to a Work Weekend, I was amazed at what it was all about."

People who come to the Chalfonte, be they volunteers, guests or staff all say the same things. They love getting to know Anne LeDuc (who owns the Chalfonte, along with Judy Bartella).

"Coming here is like coming home to family," said one guest. "A family that doesn't fight."

VOLUNTEER ARMY

Opposite: Jon Sawyer and brother Hal, whose full name is Henry W. Sawyer IV, pictured in 1984. Their great-grandfather built the Chalfonte in 1876.
Chalfonte collection

Opposite: Spackling trough and fruit on marble create a still life; discarded antique metal beds and the old boiler.

Above: Will Valentine is a dedicated weekender. He is also a history buff, writer and photographer.
Valentine collection

Above right: Harriet and Jack Riehl are Chalfonte neighbors and work weekend regulars.
Photograph by Karen Fox

Left: Nancy Dowlin, work weekender, picking crab for a wedding at the hotel.
Photograph by Judy Bartella

winter, when the hotel was shuttered, Jim was there scraping, spackling, painting and refinishing the old pine floors. He is best known for managing work weekends. It's Jim who would convene with Anne LeDuc to decide the priority projects for each work weekend, assign the volunteers and be the go-to-guy for questions and concerns.

Jim Abrams *Work Weekends Coordinator, Mount Holly, New Jersey* "Work weekends are always a team effort. We have covered over that old pea green paint many times. We have replaced toilets, windows, repaired shutters, reconstructed the Tin House, replaced gingerbread, polished floors, washed windows, gardened, repaired the kitchen. The scraping, spackling, painting never ends. I love it here despite all of the work over the more than 20 years. This place is family to me. I look forward to seeing old friends and guests and making new friends. Work weekends are energizing. It's the rhythm of getting ready for yet another season."

Jackie Brown *Columbus Grove, Ohio* "My first visit to the Chalfonte was in 1970. My husband Tracy – Trace – and I had friends who were thinking about a trip from our home in Ohio to

the coast. Diane said, 'I know this old place in New Jersey near the beach.' And we said, 'Oh, okay.' New Jersey – we never thought about visiting New Jersey, but we booked rooms at the Chalfonte for nine days, including breakfast and dinner, for $300.

"We drove for 13 hours through the night and it was perilous on the Pennsylvania Turnpike. It poured rain all night long. We arrived at the Chalfonte exhausted, and the place smelled musty and old, the humidity was high. We were shown to our rooms, and everything everywhere was a horrible pea green, and the beds were iron, chipped and rusted. I said to Trace, 'And we are going to stay here for nine days!'

"As we were unpacking, there came a knock

"The Chalfonte is a whole world in itself. The best room in the house is the Tin House. I lived there for several summers. It's a tiny room, no running water, no bathroom, but it's cool and private, like living in a dollhouse."

at the door and there was a bellman and he said that Mrs Satterfield and Mrs Nash over in the Family Hall wished for us to come over for a drink of bourbon. Now this is before lunch and I am a small town Ohio girl. I would never think of a drink before lunch, much less bourbon. I had no idea about bourbon. We accepted the invitation. The ladies were charming – passing out the bourbon and we chatted a while and before we left the room the sun came out, and the breezes floated in, wiped out the mustiness and we went on to have a wonderful time and before the week ended, we were in love with the Chalfonte and Cape May.

"It was always in the back of our minds to return to the old hotel on the coast, but we

were grounded with children and teaching and it wasn't until 1985 that we returned. And 1987 was the first of what's now 23 years of work weekends and chambermaid duties. My friend Debra and I did the work weekend, and then we called home and said we wanted to stay a week longer to help with chambermaid duties. Anne LeDuc trained me. She was thorough and precise. Now I come for the opening of the season and help train chambermaids. My husband Trace is a carpenter, an industrial tech teacher, and he has lent his skills to many projects over the years.

"I have lived all over the hotel. For several years my room was 64 — accessible only through 65 or 63, and if they were occupied, the

GREAT-GRANDSON
Opposite: Henry W. Sawyer IV is a great-grandson of the Civil War hero of the same name who opened Sawyer's Chalfonte 135 years ago. Hal Sawyer, like his great-grandfather, is a skilled carpenter.

Above: Hal and his wife Leila enjoy work weekends at the Chalfonte. Their daughters Zoe and Arden are fifth-generation Sawyers who help maintain the hotel.
Photos by Aleksey Moryakov

entrance was through a walk on the roof and a window.

"For the past nine years I have worked both ends of the summer. The chambermaid duties are 9 to 2 or 3 and that allows me my beach time. I am a beach bum and a walker. I'm 62 and toting laundry, making beds, cleaning baths are better exercise than a gym routine. It's perfect for me and all the while, I continue my love affair with the Chalfonte. This is my second home. I have made life-long friends here. Some of us sometimes gather in Mexico in winter.

"The Chalfonte is a whole world in itself. The best room in the house is the Tin House. I lived there for several summers. It's a tiny room, no running water, no bathroom, but it's cool and

private, like living in a dollhouse."

Jack and Harriet Riehl *Cape May* [Jack] "I'm a neighbor, just a couple blocks down the street from the Chalfonte. Harriet and I live in the Benton Avenue house where the hotel's builder Henry Sawyer's widow Mary McKissick Sawyer lived. This hotel is a warm place. I have worked in a lot of old buildings. The Chalfonte has a special feeling about it. It is sweet. There are seven buildings on this property and each is interesting. I'm Window Man. I clean off the shutter hardware and work the shutter dogs.

"Working on the windows, and dealing with shutters, I got the idea to create birdhouses, with encouragement from work weekender Trace Brown. They're made from discarded shutters. My wife Harriet takes apart the shutters and we lay out the pieces, including the metal fittings, hinges, hooks and pulls – and I am inspired!

MEMORY SHOT
Work weekender Will Valentine, who fondly recalls the Saturday nights after the volunteers put their tools down: "After showering and putting on some fresh clothes the intoxicating aromas of Dot and Lucille's famous fried chicken fill the hotel from the bottom up."
Valentine collection

It's creative puzzle-making putting together the pieces in houses for our feathered friends.

"Harriet and I have restored five historic houses so we feel right at home working here at the Chalfonte, built in 1876. I know how to fix those old windows that operate with weights and ropes. Working on windows is how I discovered these old shutters, some of which I think go back a 100 years and more. We use everything original in the birdhouses, including the multiple layers of paint. They've been selling like hotcakes here during work weekends when guests trade their labor of love of this old place for room and board. They can take a legitimate piece of the Chalfonte home with them. We contribute a portion of each birdhouse sale to the Chalfonte restoration fund."

Janet and Bob Dilts *Pittsburgh, Pennsylvania* [Janet] "The first time we were in Cape May

Enthusiasts Who Keep Coming Back For More

Article from *The Philadelphia Inquirer*, "Tradition at the Chalfonte Hotel – A Waiting List of Volunteers", by Dianna Marder, April 30, 2009...

CAPE MAY–Once or twice a year, Mary Paddock and her husband, Lynn, drive 700 miles from their home in Indiana, and pay $35 each to bed down on sleeping bags in unheated rooms – all for the opportunity to donate sweat equity, scraping and spackling the walls of this city's historic Chalfonte Hotel. The Paddocks, ages 70 and 71, have never been proper guests at the Chalfonte – but they have volunteered here in the off-season for nearly a dozen years.

While family obligations will keep the Paddocks away this weekend when the Chalfonte marks the first of its two May 2009 Work Weekends, many longtime volunteers are returning. Among them: Gail Angel of Churchville, Maryland, who has spent 14 years as a Chalfonte Work Weekender; Georgia Grieder, of Morris County, New Jersey, nine years; Helen Bubka, of Northeast Philadelphia, six years; and Joyce Grohman of Pomona, New Jersey, who this weekend is returning for her 16th year.

Even in Cape May, where the Chalfonte is one of many faithfully restored structures on the National Register of Historic Places, the hotel is a sight to behold. She commands almost an entire city block at Howard Street and Sewell Avenue, with her ornate, gingerbread verandas and distinctive Italianate cupola.

Still, this isn't a nonprofit. Why does this hotel keep a waiting list of folks who want to become Work Weekenders?

"We feel connected to the hotel because the hotel cherishes its connection to history," says Valerie Brown, a lawyer, lobbyist and yoga instructor in New Hope, Pennsylvania, returning for her 16th Work Weekend.

It seems the tides lure these Work Weekenders as surely as their passion for historic preservation. Some serve on their local historical societies, and others were trained as Master Gardeners by horticultural groups back home. But like parents doting on a delicate child, the volunteers are also invested in maintaining the Chalfonte's peculiar ambience.

Photograph by Will Valentine

"I feel very special helping to preserve this building that was the home of the Sawyers over a century ago. To work here is to work in a museum really, to work with people who share the same bond, have the same feelings about keeping this place alive. I learned about the Chalfonte off the internet. When I first came here I couldn't hold a hammer, could not pound in a nail. Now I'm pretty good."

we took the ferry from Lewes, Delaware and we didn't realize there was no taxi service. So we walked to town from the ferry. That's quite a hike! We walked all over town, completely charmed. When we were ready to return to the ferry, we were looking to schedule a taxi. We walked into the Chalfonte. It was such a friendly place. They helped us with a taxi, and we had a gin and tonic at the King Eddie Bar. Bob is a retired teacher and I am in real estate management and we decided we wanted to return to the Chalfonte. Work weekends allow us to do that."

Bob Dilts "I love the place. It's part of American history. I love it for Colonel Sawyer's place in military history, and to be able to be part of that. I love it for the Victorian balls and tea dances and the Secret Garden and Dot and Lucille. A lot to love, and I like helping to keep it real."

Francine & John Kelleher *Great Barrington, Massachusetts* [Francine] "We have stayed in B&Bs for a large part of our lives. We enjoyed varied experiences of cultures. We have stayed with Mennonite farmers in Lancaster, Pennsylvania with shared baths. We heard about Chalfonte work weekends on a radio show. We have been returning for work weekends for 20 years. The first weekend I washed dishes. I had the experience of working with Helen in the kitchen. She was very demanding about everything. In the off-seasons, in the spring and fall, I help with weddings."

John Kelleher "We are helping to maintain a piece of history. This is a friendly place. People who come here for work weekends are very dedicated, very willing to work hard. We have developed many friends here. The experience is very different, intriguing for educators that we are, to actually work with and live history."

Vicki O'Brien *Centerpoint, New York* "I have been work weekending since 1984. I knew nothing of Cape May. I fell in love with the Chalfonte my first weekend. It was down at the heels then. I scrape paint and spackle. For me this has become like a family reunion. There is such a sense of community here, a love of history. We who work these weekends have that same sense. And when we are not here, we correspond by email, and sometimes say, 'Oh, I got the Chalfonte blues today.'"

Julie Wood *Marlton, New Jersey* "Don't you feel the spirit here. I feel very special helping to preserve this building that was the home of the Sawyers over a century ago. To work here is to work in a museum really, to work with people who share the same bond, have the same feelings about keeping this place alive. I learned about the Chalfonte off the internet. When I first came here I couldn't hold a hammer, could not pound in a nail. Now I'm pretty good. So many important buildings are torn down. I feel a part of this location not becoming a condo. I feel I am helping keep the love of the Chalfonte contemporary as a location for concerts and family gatherings and wonderful meals. Whatever they ask you to do on a work weekend, those who come to work are willing to do housekeeping, plumbing, cooking, preparing awnings for the season. You never know what assignment you are going to get. We take pride in preserving the past for the future."

Will Valentine *Palmyra, New Jersey* [Excerpts from a Work Weekenders' Journey July, 2010] "I started my Chalfonte story by stopping for a leisurely rock on the porch after a walk around Cape May. Many porch visits later I decided to participate in a work weekend. That first weekend I helped paint the lobby and suddenly, after two days of scraping, spackling, sanding and painting a premier room in the hotel, I was no longer an outsider.

"When Anne LeDuc and Judy Bartella started the work weekends, they allowed ordinary people to participate and become a part of the Chalfonte family and its history. The expe-

rience changed me and my relationship with the hotel forever. This hotel has always been surrounded by people who love and respect it dearly, but when you become a work weekender you are part of the family that has kept the hotel going for years. Some of those years, there was concern there would not be another season.

"I have returned nearly every year since, sometimes working several weekends to scrape and paint the verandas I once rocked on when I first visited. Only now, I am an indoctrinated member of the Chalfonte family, with a scraper in hand and layers of white paint and plaster covering my clothes like a badge of honor.

"There is nothing like a Saturday night at the hotel after completing your first six hours of work. You return to your hotel room, aching and sore, as the ceiling fan above spins you into a short nap. After showering and putting on some fresh clothes the intoxicating aromas of Dot and Lucille's famous fried chicken fill the hotel from

REPAIRING HISTORY
Carpenters like Trace Brown of Ohio travel far to participate in saving a historic gem, and he's been doing it for years.

ORIGINAL STAIRCASE
Work weekender Will Valentine photographed the antique walnut staircase with oranges on the steps, just for fun.
Photographs by Will Valentine

the bottom up. The spring air blows the curtains from the windows as you comb your hair in the pitted silver of a Victorian mirror and the experience transcends the work.

"The hotel may be hosting a Saturday evening event – a wedding or I recall with fondness Victorian ballroom dancers arriving in full costume, with a live chamber quartet filling the hotel with music of the sort that Henry Sawyer himself would have danced to. I chose to sit in the Queen Anne room off the lobby, with a glass of wine, listening to the music, enjoying the glow of lamplight beyond the porches.

"Last year at summer's end I treated myself as a guest in room 40, one I had helped paint a few years earlier. The difference now is that it was air conditioned, thanks to new owner Bob Mullock and family. The Mullocks work right alongside work weekenders, painting and scraping and getting to know the veterans of many seasons."

CHAPTER VII

Perennial Guests: Naughty & Nice

AS SURELY as the hydrangeas and the roses emerge each season at the Chalfonte, the guests who come year after year – the perennials – are the Chalfonte's lifeblood. The perennials are a micro-culture, enjoying summertime in its purest: salty seas, wispy breezes, billowing sheers, rocking chair rhythms, story telling, singing, lots of fresh foods and strong spirits, as in a glass. They have no use for nonessentials that complicate their reverence for – and practice of – simpler times.

The Chalfonte for more than 130 years had no air conditioning, no television, no computer hookups and mostly hallway shared baths. There were no double beds or bar until 1978. Cocktail parties were held in rooms and The Playroom which also served as an impromptu theater.

For the perennials, summers at the Chalfonte mark time and evoke timelessness: the gathering of generations, families and friends, for reunions to rejuvenate, to mourn, to celebrate birthdays, weddings, births. It is a very special connectedness that only the Chalfonte porches, lobby, dining tables and Tin House cocktail parties provide – a going home to the lacey old Valentine.

John W. Alexander is a perennial. He's been summering at the Chalfonte for more than 70 years. His father, John Sr, proposed to his sweetheart, Rosalie Jones, on one of the second floor Romeo and Juliet balconies in the late 1920s. The Alexanders returned annually after their marriage in 1930 with young sons, Greg and John Jr, aka Johnno. (The name Johnno was invented after the Alexanders were smitten with the movie *The Informer*, starring Victor McLaglen, the hero, who was called Gypo.)

Johnno met his sweetheart though a Chalfonte connection. Johno was acquainted with James (Jimmy) Morris, Meenie Satterfield's nephew. Jimmy said, "Our friend Leslie Bullington of Richmond is in Philadelphia. Can you introduce her to some of your younger friends?"

"I did call Leslie, met her and kept her for myself," says Johnno. "Ironically she had gone to St Catherine's in Richmond with Nancy Satterfield and Maria Carter [Satterfield], but Leslie

THE CHALFONTE
CAPE MAY, NEW JERSEY

NOTICE TO GUESTS
The hotel is not responsible for the loss of valuables, unless deposited in the safe, provided for that purpose, in the office.

Bathing from rooms permitted
Only under the following conditions

1. Positively no bathing suits may be rinsed in baths, basins or showers.
2. Guests will *please* use the *shower* provided at the *bath house* in the rear for removing *all sand* from their suits, feet, etc., before coming in to the hotel.
THIS MOST IMPORTANT
3. Guests in bathing suits are requested not to come on the front porch or in the lobby.
Guests are requested to be quiet in the halls at night, also in their rooms.
Maids will sit on the side porches.
Children under five years not allowed in the large dining room.
Children must not run and romp in the halls and on porches.
Quiet hour is from 3 to 5 P. M. Please cooperate with us in observing this rest hour.
Dogs not allowed.
Guests are requested not to play cards in the lobby on Sunday.

HOURS FOR MEALS

BREAKFAST	8:30 to 9:30
DINNER	1:30 to 2:30
SUPPER	6:30 to 7:30

1 Bell	Ice Water
2 Bells	Bell Man
3 Bells	Chambermaid
4 Bells	Porter
5 Bells	Hot Water

NOTICE TO GUESTS
This sign was posted in every room for decades. Note that maids are only allowed to sit on the side porches. Quiet hour was 3-5pm: "Please cooperate with us in observing this rest hour." And guests couldn't play cards in the lobby on Sunday.
John Alexander

FABULOUS FIFTIES
Previous page: Jim and Margaret Grove fell in love at the hotel – they couldn't get enough of Cape May beaches and Chalfonte hospitality.
Margaret Grove

had never been to the Chalfonte, so that was my pleasure to introduce her to the old hotel."

Like his parents, Johnno and Leslie have shared years of Chalfonte summertime with their children Emily, Caroline and John III, who worked as a bellman. "My brother Greg's daughters, Julia and Mary Beth, they are all Chalfontians."

John Alexander Jr *Bryn Mawr, Pennsylvania* "When I was in college, if you went to the Chalfonte as a student, you took advantage of Meenie's Three Hots and a Cot – three meals and a cot for $15 a week. There were a dozen cots in the King Edward Suite – now the bar. The cots were said to be surplus from the Spanish-American War. We had to dress up for breakfast, and there was one sink for a dozen guys. There was a lot of jostling. William, the head waiter, stood

poised to shut the dining room door at precisely 9:30am. It was William's power moment. There was no bargaining despite a stampede of freshly shaved men dashing to the door.

"I've thought over the years the Chalfonte looks like a Mississippi riverboat, somehow high and dry at Howard and Sewell. I have memories from seven decades.

"The 30s: My father dressing in a coat and tie for breakfast after ringing five bells for hot water. There was a placard on the back of the bedroom door: one bell for ice, two bells for the bell man, three bells of the chambermaid, four bells for the porter. The hot water arrived in a big pitcher. Father decanted the water in a porcelain basin and shaved. I remember nurse maids feeding their charges in the Children's Dining Room. I'll never forget commuting from the hotel through

SUMMER TRADITION
Above: The Alexander family of the Philadelphia Main Line has been summering at the Chalfonte for more than 70 years. Photographed at the Tin House, August, 1939 are John W. "Johno" Alexander Jr, left, his mother Rosalie, baby Gregory and father John. Top right: Rosalie and John were engaged at the Chalfonte and after their marriage returned for summer fun. They are pictured in 1939 at the Stockton Baths where hotel guests dressed for the beach and showered.
John Alexander

alleys and side yards to the Stockton Baths on the beachfront. There were no beach services at the hotel and all the undressing and dressing happened at the bathhouse, always mindful of being properly dressed for meals.

"The 40s: Army and Navy wives crowding the hotel in war time. The overflow being accommodated at Miss Browne's on Howard Street. Long family-style tables. Dinner from 1:30 to 2:30 and a rigidly-enforced quiet time from 3pm to 5pm.

"The 50s: The lobby shows on Saturday night of Labor Day weekend featuring Ty Mudge, Harry Rhein and Marie Zara Randall, author of "The Chalfonte Song," and Bellman Henry Thatch in a supporting role. Movie star Veronica Lake's visit to the Chalfonte. The all-summer guests Marian Taylor, Miss Reannie, Mary Sattler, Ruth Owen, Mae Stevens. The beach picnics at Higbee on the bay, featuring hotel handyman Theodore Roosevelt Jackson cooking huge lobsters in tins over an open fire until deliciously tender. Theodore obtained enormous lobsters from A. J. Seafood Market for $1 to $2 a pound. Before the King Eddie Bar, guests would give parties in their rooms complete with Planters Peanuts, chips and Tom Collins mix from McCray's Market.

"The 60s: Staff changes with the teen children of guests and their friends becoming wait-

WESTERN UNION TELEGRAM

W. P. MARSHALL, PRESIDENT

1201

The filing time shown in the date line on domestic telegrams is STANDARD TIME at point of origin. Time of receipt is STANDARD TIME at point of destination

`. AUG 6  AM 10 02`   (00)

PA14 RD033

R LLB072 PD= RICHMOND VIR 6 948AME=

CHARLES A ROSE=

CARE MRS KNOX WILSON HOTEL CHALFONTE CAPEMAY NJER=

= ROOM AVAILABLE HERE IF NEEDED=

MOTHER=

WESTERN UNION TELEGRAM

W. P. MARSHALL, PRESIDENT

The filing time shown in the date line on domestic telegrams is STANDARD TIME at point of origin. Time of receipt is STANDARD TIME at point of destination

`. JUL 1201 AM`

PA004 SPV045 BA729

B YXG081 NL PD=PH NEW YORK NY 6=

MRS MENIE SATTERFIELD=

CHALFONTE HTL CAPE MAY NJER=

WE ARRIVED TODAY AND GOT YOUR CORDIAL LETTER HOWEVER ANITA IS SO EXHAUSTED AND IN SO MUCH PAIN WE HAVE TO GO STRAIGHT BACK TO SAN FRANCISCO AS SOON AS WE CAN GET AIRPLANE RESERVATIONS SO WE CANNOT SEE YOU NOR JOHN AND HIS FAMILY THIS IS A BITTER DISAPPOINTMENT=

A B COURT=.

The Penn Albert HOTEL
GREENSBURG, PA.

JOHN A. SHEETZ Manager

AMPLE PARKING

May 31, 1959

Mrs. Satterfield
The Chalfonte
Cape May, New Jersey:

Dear Mrs. Satterfield:

I hope you will find room for me on the third floor - no bath, but across the hall from one - for the 4th of July weekend, Friday July 3 to 6th inclusive.

Still using most of my vacation for ski trips - and we just can't s in the summer.

Regards to everyone.

Sincerely yours,

Charles Beierschmitt
Penn Albert Hotel
Greensburg, Penna.

---

ers and waitresses. And keys for the first time to the previously all-keyless Chalfonte. Costume and theme parties in The Playroom and lobby. Transfusions before lunch: one-third vodka, one-third beef bouillon, one-third tomato juice and lemon juice, Worcestershire, Tabasco and horseradish to taste. We gathered for Transfusions on the porch at Room 30 in the Annex, usually occupied by Harry and Marge Strater of Louisville. After-dinner Stingers, a combination of brandy and white crème de menthe, in the Playroom. We all chipped in for the ingredients and tips for the bellman. I don't know how we ate all the big meals and drank all those fancy drinks. If you drank too much, you were 'Chalfontized'. Parties were sometimes called 'porch

BY WIRE AND LETTER
Since there was only one telephone in the Chalfonte, in a booth, off the lobby, communication was by telegram and letter.
Chalfonte collection

BEACH FUN
Opposite: Friends of Sally Mead, and Chalfonte guests, enjoy the sun and sand of Cool Cape May.
Mead family collection

falls' [for the risk involved], a term popularized by Joe Barker in his unique publication *Pennywise*. Piano music and nightcaps with the Chalfonte crowd at Henri's on the Beach. Nancy Satterfield Davey provided West Side Story sheet music for pianist Bobby Harris so whenever the Chalfonte crowd entered, Bobby would roll into 'Maria', 'I Feel Pretty', 'Tonight'.

"The 70s and 80s: Vacationing with my wife and our family and finding that they love the Chalfonte, too – now a third generation of

Alexanders to do so.

"The 90s: My son John becomes a hotel staff member.

"The 2000s: Still enjoying the special Chalfonte magic, although there are too many late friends' names on the porch rockers."

* * *

Three young Army men – Robert (Sully) Sullivan, Sondy Sonderskov and Jim Grove – met during the Korean War and remained friends. The Chalfonte became their gathering place, a hub of their lives, and to this day their families gather at the hotel as they have for more than 50 years. Sully and Sondy were boyhood classmates in Champagne, Illinois and ended up in the same Army unit, where they met Jim Grove of Charlottesville, Virginia. Jim's sister, Mary "Grovie" Boylan, was a member of the dining room staff. When the three Army buddies decided to get together, Jim suggested his friends, now in New York City, meet him at the Chalfonte. That initial visit evolved into a trio of romances, engagements, marriages, families and a continuum of second and third generations coming home to the Chalfonte for summer vacations – and romance.

Robert (Sully) Sullivan *New York City, New York* "I first visited the Chalfonte in 1958, and I have returned at least once a summer ever since. I have been a Chalfonte regular for over half a century. I courted my wife Merrinelle here. Merrinelle was from Little Rock, Arkansas. She went to Stephens College in Missouri, then moved to New York City with two phone numbers, two suitcases and $200. One of the phone numbers was Nancy Satterfield's – she also had attended Stephens. They roomed together in New York and later on, Merrinelle roomed with Anne LeDuc at Gramercy Park. Merrinnelle spent weekends at the Chalfonte, and worked here. We became engaged here, and married in 1960. My daughters, Amanda and Susan, spent their childhood summers at the Chalfonte.

"We had a circle of friends from New York and Baltimore and we would arrange to come at the same time. The impromptu parties, the costume performances were legendary. I especially was charmed by Martha Nash, the petite linens' lady, appearing in a tutu as a ballerina. Clever guests created theme parties and came dressed in strange get-ups. Seemed to me to be a never-ending series of masquerade parties. Transfusions – a form of a Bloody Mary

From The Archives

Excerpt from The Chalfonte Newsletter 1978...

EDITORIAL

As spring bursts forth, we look ahead with heightened spirits to 1978 and to more long-range restoration plans to insure our family-style hotel.

We have many hopes and plans, which, of course, include Helen and Dot and the Tin House reunions, etc. You will rock in firmer rocking chairs this year. Hopefully you will be greeted by a new green awning. There will be new carpeting in some of the rooms. There are 20 new mattresses – double beds – a Chalfonte first! A new lounge, The King Edward Suite, will enable you to have that cool draft beer en route from the beach, or sip your stingers after dinner in air-conditioned splendor. There may even be a Chalfonte laundry out back. The bathrooms may surprise you, and the lobby is getting a "face lifting." Gone are the "pea green" walls. Meenie and Martha join us in looking forward to seeing you all again this summer.

– were an institution here before lunch, before there was any bar here. It was a drink that led to mirth and merry-making at mid-day.

"One season someone decided to have a Cape May-New York party, in New York. Martha Nash was famous for counting all the sheets and towels. It was her obsession. A couple weeks before the party, lady friends of Martha and Meenie gathered up Chalfonte towels, sheets, tablecloths, napkins, cutlery, china. When Martha and Meenie were welcomed in New York and fawned over with great ceremony, they were shocked speechless about the dining table, the bedrooms and baths all dressed in Chalfonte possessions. Once they caught their breath there was great hilarity.

Amanda Sullivan *New York City, New York* I have been summering at the Chalfonte all my life. When I was a little girl my mother paid me a dime for every cigarette butt I picked up along the Annex porch. I could drink all the Cokes I wanted and enjoyed a steady diet of Tab and warm biscuits. I ate my favorite, grits with lots of butter, every day. Like the children of other Chalfonte regulars, I worked at the hotel, first as a manager of the Children's Dining Room, working up to manager of the Magnolia Room in 1996. I also did some PR for the hotel, and worked in the kitchen. Chapters of my life have evolved here. I was engaged here, married here and celebrated the births of my three children here." [See Chapter XI for Amanda's wedding story.]

Margaret Grove *Charlottesville, Virginia* "Jim and I were good friends in Charlottesville. Jim had been dating a friend of mine, and he was well known to my family. When Jim asked my father's permission for me to take a drive with him to Cape May and the Chalfonte to visit his sister, Grovie Boylan, who was working there, my father did not hesitate. It was all right. Now the drive is seven hours. When we arrived well after midnight, there was a party going on. There was a string in the lobby, and a sign saying, 'Follow Me.' The string led to a party on the second floor. We had so much fun with the Chalfonte crowd, we stayed 11 days. Jim and I fell in love while in Cape May. We also fell in love with the Chalfonte and all the wonderful friends we have met here and continue to see. Our first visit was in 1953. We were married the next September and we have been coming ever since. My son and his friends worked here and now my son brings his family here. We all love the

Sullivan Family Album

The Sullivans of New York City have stories of engagements, a wedding, birth celebrations – all at their beloved Chalfonte. Top: Sully (second from left) the night he met his future wife. Top right: Merrinelle's formal engagement photo circa 1959. Above: Merrinelle and Sully one summer's evening at the Chalfonte. Right: The Sullivans' daughter Amanda at age three. She spent every childhood summer at the hotel, worked there, married there, and now visits with her husband and children.

Chalfonte. It is a different sort of atmosphere. My friends get curious about the lifestyle here because I am always so excited to be returning. They wanted to come too. I say, 'Oh, no, you won't like it. It's very unusual. No phones, no TV, no air conditioning, shared hall baths.' But some came anyway, and they love it, too."

John Grove *Needham, Massachusetts, son of Jim and Margaret* "I have visited the Chalfonte once a summer since I was three or four years old. In 1980, out of high school, some of my buddies came up and worked on and off at the hotel for five full summers, through graduate school. Anne LeDuc would come down to Charlottesville and interview 20 to 30 of my college buddies. Half the Chalfonte staff would come up from Charlottesville. One summer half of my fraternity from UVA worked here. I worked as a bellman and in maintenance. I have always been interested in architecture and have always loved the building. As a kid at 18, I thought I was never going to experience this again. All together at one place, my family, my college buddies. This is as good as it gets, this way of life here. They say you can't go home. Well, we who have experienced the Chalfonte can go home.

THE EATING'S GOOD
For many years the main meal at the Chalfonte was at lunch time. If guests went to the beach before noon, they showered at Stockton baths and returned, dressed for "dinner" and a famous drink at the hotel, called the Transfusion.
Mead collection

NATIONAL PROFILE
Opposite: A 1950s article in *Life* magazine was not entirely complimentary, but times were tough and Meenie Satterfield was glad for the publicity. Meenie is quoted saying, "Nothing works. But the guests keep coming back. They feel a great loyalty to it. The ceiling could fall on their heads and they wouldn't say anything. They're nice people."
Phoebe Peyton Hanson

That is the beauty of the continuity of the place.

"There are no TVs and no phones and that makes you come out on the porch and talk and tell stories. The place is about conversation and communicating and the Chalfonte community.

"I moved to Boston and was finally able to be a paying guest. I booked a room, and Anne explained that the hotel was full, and it was a special situation, and she placed me in the Much Hots Room. Have you heard the story about the Much Hots Room? The Much Hots Room was a windowless room off the Family Hall and during Susie Satterfield's reign an Asian nursemaid stayed in the room. Susie asked her, 'And, how do you like your room?' And the nursemaid said, 'Much hots, much hots.'"

John's wife Kate and two step-children, Charlie and Anna, vacation at the Chalfonte and have learned to love it. Charlie thinks the cupola is magical.

Sondy Sonderskov *New York City, New York* "I felt at home here instantly. As we were driving here this weekend, I knew that it would be the same arriving here; that we would live again as if it were 40 years ago.

"Theodore and Henry, the handyman and

On a sunny day, shadows play on The Chalfonte's filigreed balconies, but not much else happens.

The Chalfonte

Cape May, on the southern end of New Jersey, has been a popular resort for more than a hundred years. It has one of the finest collections of late Victorian frame buildings along the eastern seaboard. The summer people who go there now are amused by the gingerbready hotels. They prefer to stay, however, in more modern accommodations. The Chalfonte is only three blocks from the water, but most of its guests seldom get to the beach, preferring to rock quietly in the front parlor. "Mostly they just want a place to relax," says the owner. "The building's a specimen of the living past. Nothing works. But the guests keep coming back. They feel a great loyalty to it. The ceiling could fall on their heads and they wouldn't say anything. They're *nice* people."

Built in 1872 by a Civil War veteran, the Chalfonte Hotel is one of the most graceful remnants of New Jersey Vict... summer the reg... increasingly olde...

Margaret Grove's 80th birthday party at the Chalfonte

Susan Satterfield Neligan

Margaret 's grandchildren Charlie and Anna Bateman

Judy Bartella

Amanda Sullivan

The birthday girl gets goofy

Margaret Grove and Nancy Granick

The Chalfonte's famous willow tree, site of many a happy moment. It was planted by Luigi Dickerson, Helen's husband.

Cricket Satterfield, Jimmy Morris, Calvin Satterfield IV

Edward Zeme and Stacy Douglas

Sondy Sonderskov and John Grove

Mary and Walker Taylor

At the King Eddie Bar: Jimmy Morris, Pat Satterfield, Jane Morris, John and Leslie Alexander, Cricket Satterfield

the bellman, these southern major domos, functioned in a way that does not exist anymore. The lifestyle at this hotel is unavailable anywhere else in the world and it was that way for many years. Meenie and Helen brought their cultural two worlds together. They understood each other and embraced each other and each other's families and stood together and created and sustained this very special high southern form of civilization. Their dedication to each other generated the stage that we all have enjoyed so much. Their dedication to each other is why this building still stands today, a living monument of history and architecture and combining of cultures.

"Sully and I were in second grade together, we were in the same unit in the Army. Jim Grove became our friend of a lifetime. Jim Grove had tremendous perception, a booming laugh, a wonderful sense of humor. Jim has passed, but we all remember him as fresh as yesterday."

Meredith Fuller Sonderskov "Bob [Sondy] and I met Labor Day weekend 1978. I was in my knitting shop in Baltimore and it was hot as blue blazes. Mother called and said it was much cooler in Cape May. I said, 'Mother, I have all these boxes of yarn to unpack.' She said, 'That's silly. Come to cool Cape May.' I went home, packed a bathing suit, and was at the Chalfonte in time for dinner. We went to a movie, walked the boardwalk, and on returning someone said, 'We've got a new bartender from New York. He's an actor, in New York theater.' We went in the bar, sat down, and you could hear his booming voice all over the room. I noted how tall he was. The next day he said, 'Aren't you coming to the beach?' I thought, what a bossy thing you are. I had lunch, took a nap before going to the beach. He said, 'Well, it took you long enough.' He said to call if ever I got to New York. I went to a wool market in October. I called and he said I want to take you to dinner. We went to dinner and to a club dancing, and noon the next day he called and said, 'We belong together.' We were together for 19 years, and married June 28th, 1997. My mother and father, Nancy and Lawrence Fuller, before me loved the Chalfonte. They were great friends of Meenie. My great-aunt Elizabeth, a well-known impressionist artist, loved the spoonbread and fish for breakfast, the kidney stew and hot biscuits."

Jimmy Morris *Richmond, Virginia* "My father, Jimmy Morris, had a bad leg and was ineligible for the war. He was an auditor for the state of

From The Archives

Excerpt from The Chalfonte Newsletter, Summer 1978...

July 22 – BROADWAY THEATRE PARTY: Producer Al Partenheimer, stars too numerous to mention. Dance (or hum) to theatre music; presenting the Bi-Annual "Meenie Awards," superb "off-Broadway" entertainment. Come as a character out of a Broadway show – prizes for most authentic, most original, most comic (adult and child divisions).

July 29 – CLOSE ENCOUNTERS OF THE CHALFONTE KIND: A Celestial Ball, a party of star gazers and a true trip to outer space (if there is any in the playroom)! Moon drinks, fortune tellers, light festival. Come act out your fantasies... Dress out of this world. Surprise guest – a robot.

August 12 – CHALFONTE VARIETY SHOW. Bring your talent (and a costume) – sing, act, entertain. Prizes for most original, best performance, best supporting character (adults and children). Singing waiters and waitresses.

LABOR DAY, SEPT. 1-4. The usual last fling with beach picnic Sunday.

Virginia and after Meenie's husband died, he ran the Chalfonte business, developed guest card and bookkeeping systems.

"I spent three summers here during the war. I played baseball with the local boys, bicycled all over town, searched for tar balls on the beach from ships sunk off the coast. I recall lights out and when the war ended, the VE Day celebration in the Playroom.

"My wife Jane and I honeymooned here, in Room 40, the premiere suite with the bathtub with the feet. That was 53 years ago this week [June, 2010].

"My friend Johno [Alexander] always wore bow ties. He was proud to be a member of the Philadelphia Troop, of the Union Side in the Civil War. When he married Leslie from Richmond he didn't wear his troop button any longer.

"One night we got to drinking and Sat, quite the athlete, was boasting about his tennis game. Anne LeDuc challenged him to a duel at the tennis club. Bets were made all around. The match took place with a raucous betting crowd from the Chalfonte in attendance. Let me say that Anne soundly whipped Sat's butt and it humbled him – for a few days.

"Quiet Hour was an institution. Guests took naps every afternoon. We undressed and dressed for the beach at the Stockton Baths. Then undressed and dressed for lunch and imbibed in Transfusions, then undressed for the nap, then perhaps dressing again for the beach, undressing and showering and dressing for supper at night.

"I contemplated introducing my children to the Chalfonte. We are driving up from Virginia, and I explained, this hotel is not really on the ocean. There is no air conditioning, there are no elevators, there is no lock on your door, there are no TVs or telephones. My children said, 'Well then why are we going. Let's turn around and go home.' They had no great expectation, but the magic caught on, and they loved it like all the rest of us.

"*Life* magazine did a picture story on America's famous hotels in the 1950s, and the Chalfonte was among them. Even though it was negative, saying that 'nothing works, but the guests keep coming back,' it was a boost for Meenie's business. Meenie's birthday was Bastille Day, July 14th. Jane and I came to see her on her 80th birthday. She had two Black Russians, walked straight up those many stair steps to her bedroom. She was unsinkable."

RATE CHART

The Chalfonte

301 Howard Street
Cape May, N.J. 08204

(609) 884-8934

DAILY:

Single with running water, second floor . .	$22.00
Single with running water, third floor . . .	20.00
Single without running water, second floor	19.00
Single without running water, third floor .	17.00
Double with running water, second floor .	40.00
Double with running water, third floor . .	36.00
Double without running water	33.00
Double with private bath, second floor . .	47.00
Double with private bath, third floor . . .	44.00
2 doubles, connecting bath, second floor .	85.00
2 doubles, connecting bath, third floor . .	78.00

WEEKLY:

Single with running water, second floor . .	126.00
Single with running water, third floor . . .	114.00
Single without running water, second floor	108.00
Single without running water, third floor .	96.00
Double with running water, second floor .	228.00
Double with running water, third floor . .	208.00
Double with private bath, second floor . .	270.00
Double with private bath, third floor	252.00
Doubles without running water	192.00
2 doubles connecting bath, second floor .	486.00
2 doubles connecting bath, third floor . . .	444.00

No singles with private bath
Above rates include breakfast and dinner
(Modified American plan)
Lunch available if desired (additional charge)
No Sunday evening meal served
Extra cot or crib in room . . . . per day $12.50
per week $72.00
Meal charges for transients Breakfast - $2.75
Sunday breakfast $3.00   Dinner - $6.25
Gratuities not included.

Bill Tyler *Atlanta, Georgia* "The year is 1954, the place is Louisville, Kentucky, and my younger brother Terry and I contracted polio, the dreaded crippling epidemic that year, as vaccines against it were being tested. He was four and I was seven and we went through treatment and had some residual muscle atrophy, my left leg, and his right arm. The medical people said what would be best for these children is to take them to the beach all summer, and have them walk in the sand to strengthen their legs. Now where would this destination be? It's going to be summer and it's going to be a place for a family of modest means and in the north.

"My parents were acquainted with Marge

CHANGING STYLES
Top: A Sunday on the Chalfonte porch in the 1970s, with some skirts getting shorter, while other ladies still wore hats, gloves and pumps.

A PRIZED LUXURY
Until recently private baths and tubs were rare in Chalfonte rooms. You'll note from the rate chart that most rooms had just a sink.
Chalfonte collection

and Harry Strater, who were Chalfonte regulars. On their recommendation we summered at the Chalfonte for four or five seasons. There was the beach for our physical routines, the Children's Dining Room for our meals and the bar for mother. It was an ideal situation.

"My father Sam, a traveling paint salesman, came up a couple times a summer. He became fast friends with Jim Wheat and the Satterfields. I became friends with the Campbells – Ron and Jule – and close with Anne LeDuc. Later, when I went to Camp Dudley in upstate New York, Anne would meet my plane in New York, show me the city, and put me on the milk train to camp.

Another Special Day At The Chalfonte

Excerpts from a journal kept by Christine Murphy, of Doylestown, Pennsylvania, August 2, 2003

I rose with the dawn. The sun was just barely visible from my window. I tiptoed and put on my shorts, packed my journal and camera and headed down the Chalfonte stairs. It is hard to be quiet going down stairs 100-plus years old.

I loved the little table by the window, sun coming in, a fresh flower greeting me against the white tablecloth. So simple, yet so lovely. Hot coffee, fresh blueberries and strawberries, wonderful little biscuits, fried fish, spoon bread, scrambled eggs, bacon, and I was very lucky – fried tomatoes. I lingered, just taking in the view .

I pulled a rocking chair to face the morning sun and read my paper. The porch is a great place to do some creative writing, dabble in poetry, maybe get out my paint set.

The noon whistle blew across the island and I was reminded how quickly time passes by.

***

It was nice to come back, climb the Chalfonte stairs to my room, and take a brief rest on my bed, a cotton quilt at the bottom, the sea breeze blowing the lace curtains and all my warm memories of childhood summers at the shore came drifting through those curtains.

***

Around 6pm I bid adieu to the ocean, the warmth of the sand, the descending sun, packed up my towel and beach chair and made my way along Howard Street. People were assembled on the porch waiting for the dining room to open. I snuck back to the clanging ice machine and with a bucket of ice climbed the stairs. I sipped an excellent scotch on the second-floor porch, the flag waving in the breeze, watched the setting sun, smelled the ocean, listened to the laughter of children on the sidewalk below.

As I dressed for dinner, I heard clomp-clomp of a horse, reminding me of days gone by. For a moment in time, I was living in the Victorian Age.

The maitre d' led me to a charming table overlooking the Secret Garden. I ordered a cup of clam chowder, the salad of the day and... roast beef with roasted potatoes and green beans.

***

I walked out on the porch to animated conversations, and the creaking of rocking chairs against old wooden planks. Street lanterns lighted my way as I strolled toward the ocean. There, the most magnificent moon shared its light over the vast sea below.

Right: Room 43, the largest in the hotel.
Chalfonte collection

"When I was a college freshman, I asked Anne for a job. She said, 'Okay, you have the job, if you bring four or five of your friends to work with you.' Anne contributed her life, soul and money to create the great Chalfonte atmosphere. It's not easy being the social chairman – and, the plumber.

"There were wonderful characters: Henry, the bellman, whose ritual greeting was, 'On behalf of the Hotel Association of America, we welcome you to the famous Chalfonte.' He knew everything about everything, a predecessor to Google.

"And Theodore, the handyman worth his weight in gold, with his little private room that had a mysterious odor. Even the most naive among us knew it was the marijuana that made him so happy. Let us not forget the infamous peephole between the men and women's stalls in the outdoor showers.

"Later on, I introduced my family, my youngsters Meg and Will, to the Chalfonte. They loved it and the reason they did is since there is no TV, you give 100 percent of your attention to them."

Katie Kiliani Bliss *Maplewood, New Jersey* "The year was 1958. My family lived in Pittsburgh. Our wonderful family times at the Chalfonte were the result of tragedy. My older brother died of cancer, and my mother needed a place to go, a comfortable and safe place to be away from everything. A friend suggested the Chalfonte, and that sounded good to Mother because there was a Children's Dining Room. I was three years old and my brother was five, and mother was pregnant. Apparently I was an energetic three--year-old, because I had no fear of the waves. I kept running out to meet them, and mother, being pregnant, couldn't get up easily to chase after me. Anne LeDuc took over on the beach and she became my second mother.

"I call the Chalfonte my happy place. It became my family's summer place. We vacationed there every year for a week or two. We always stayed in the same rooms – 63, 64, 65 at the top of the stairs near the Family Wing. Like so many other children of guests I started working at the hotel when I was 18. I wanted to be just like Cathy McConnan who was in charge of the Children's Dining Room when I was a little one. She was my hero. In the summers of 1974, 75, 77 – I had moved to New York and I would take the bus down every weekend to the Chalfonte to be with friends and work. Then, of course, when you got serious about someone, that per-

A Notable Visitor

A hotel guest the summer of 2010 was Chalfonte builder Henry Sawyer's great-great-grandson, Harold G. Knight Jr of Bethesda, Maryland.

As is his tradition, Knight invited his wife Deborah on a weekend with a surprise destination. He made arrangements to take the Cape May-Lewes Ferry with reservations at the Chalfonte. "I wanted to see the new renovations," he said.

Knight's grandmother was born at the hotel in 1883, the daughter of Henry and Harriet Sawyer's daughter Louisa. As a boy Knight spent summers in and around the hotel, walking there from his grandmother Louisa Ware's house on Hughes Street, near Jefferson.

He always has been fascinated with the history of his great-great-grandfather, the Civil War hero. The Chalfonte is a special place for Harold and his family, and he hopes to spend more time there again, now that he's retired.

son had to pass the Chalfonte test. I took Mark down in 1980. He had worked for a contractor, and Mrs Satterfield asked him to do some work on a wall by the Solarium. When it was time to go back to New York after the weekend, he said, 'I'm not going back. I'm going to stay and finish this wall.' And, of course, that endeared him to Meenie. She said, 'I do declare, this is the best wall in the building.' My husband proposed to me there, after he and my dad took a walk, and he got my parents' permission. The Chalfonte is a family inn. We are now in a third generation. My children work there – Genie is a waitress and bartender, and Taylor worked the front desk this past season."

* * *

Christine Murpy has been returning to the Chalfonte for 20 years. In the 50s, she vacationed in Cape May with her parents at Congress Hall and the Christian Admiral. In the summer of 1991, she was considering returning to Cape May and a friend suggested the Chalfonte.

Christine Murphy *Doylestown, Pennsylvania* "When life takes difficult turns (two bouts of cancer and downsizing of jobs), I know if I get to this porch I will be okay. I love being around people. Here you can be entirely by yourself, or join in, and this has become a second family for me. My routine is luxury: beach in the morning, writing in my journals, walking around town taking photos, updating my albums, vegging out. It's a lifestyle that's just right for me."

Cindy & George Waters & daughter Caitlin *Falls Church, Virginia* [Cindy] "We were looking to go to a different beach and we read in the food section of the *Washington Post* about Helen in the Chalfonte kitchen and the southern food. So we tried it out. This is in 1982 and we got to our room, and we thought, 'Oh, God, this is awful.' The sink was dripping and there was a bare lightbulb and no lock on the door.

"We thought about finding another place to stay. Then we got to the beach and it was nice and we were invited to a Tin House party. We met Anne and Judy and they were so nice, and Anne said, 'Oh, you have the worst room in the hotel. Come back next year, and we will assure a better room.

"We brought our seven-month-old baby girl Caitlin here in 1992. And here we are 28 years later from our first visit, and Caitlin has met girls her own age, and they are fast friends and they are planning on their own rooms for next year. Caitlin looks forward to each season. The

GANG'S ALL HERE
A typical gathering of the Satterfield family and Chalfonte perennial guests and hotel staff at the Tin House circa 1971.
Chalfonte collection

girls call themselves the Howard Street Mafia. All the girls will be going off to college this year.

"We met Dick Sattler here the first year and he has become a life-long friend, though his antics are hard to take."

Dick Sattler *St Louis, Missouri* "Cindy worked for a US Senator in Washington. I called for Cindy one day, and the Senator answered the phone. He said, 'Who may I say is calling?' and I said, 'Just tell her Cannonball called.' The Senator is Bill Cohen of Maine who later became Secretary of Defense. He said to Cindy, 'You just had a call from Mr Cannonball.'

"My family rented houses in the neighborhood and when I was about 12, I started working at the Chalfonte. I had a little wagon and they'd send me to the liquor store for the day's supply. I needed to make several trips.

"My father was in the underwear manufacturing business. He had boxes of women's underwear. When I was a boy, I sold underwear to all the women in the hotel, and from my wagon around the neighborhood. No, I didn't have to pay for the underwear. There was no overhead – all profit."

George Waters "Some years ago there was a prominent West Virginia judge experiencing

a first visit at the Chalfonte. He wrote a card to his friend that said, 'This is the damdest hotel you have ever seen. You have to wear a jacket to breakfast, but take a shower out back in the field.'

"There have been enough people conceived here to populate a town the size of Cape May."

Ron Campbell was art director at *Fortune* magazine. His wife Jule produced the first *Sports Illustrated* swimsuit edition in 1964, famous for making the bikini acceptable beach wear in the US. The five-page layout on a Cozumel beach was so successful that Jule was assigned annually to scout models and exotic locations for the swimsuit editions. Jule became a powerhouse in the fashion world, choosing larger, healthy, athletic looking models and the best beaches of the world for the shoots. Jule Campbell made the *SI* swimsuit issue into the largest money-making machine at *Sports Illustrated*. She excelled in that unique editor's position until 1996. During her 32-year tenure she hand-picked beauties who would become supermodels, including Christie Brinkley, Cheryl Tiegs, Carol Alt, Kathy Ireland and many more.

Jule knew Nancy Satterfield Davey from their school days at Stephens College. When

Jule suggested they break away and spend some beach time in Cape May, Ron was expecting an informal place, amid sea grass, right on the beach. He packed shorts, casual slacks and sports shirts – certainly no ties. Much to Ron's shock, the Chalfonte was a dowdy Victorian, with dinner jackets mandatory at communal dining tables. Meenie and Martha, old south fashionistas, sometimes fussed about Jule's fashion sense. Little did they know she would become an international fashion icon.

The Campbells could vacation anywhere in the world, but year after year they choose the Chalfonte.

Ron Campbell & Jule Campbell, son Bruce, grandson Graham *New York City, New York & Flemington, New Jersey* [Jule] "We've been going to the Chalfonte for almost 50 years. Our first time, our son Bruce was five years old. We arrive and there is no bellman available. We're told our rooms are on the second floor of the Howard

JURASSIC LARK
They have been a lot of unusual guests at Chalfonte but none quite like Rex, the dinosaur, part of a week-long series of fun for children in 1996.
Photograph by Judy Bartella

Street Cottage next door. Actually the rooms were on the third floor, and we toted our luggage up the steps and water is trickling down the steps. A bathtub has overflowed.

"Our room is unmade, bedding and pillows askew. My husband says, 'Good God, what is this? Three fingers of scotch, now! And I am not staying here!' Ronnie says it loudly, and I say, 'Sssshhhhttt, these are friends of mine, quiet!'

"There are several children running around having fun and we learn they are the Eastburn family of New Hope, Pennsylvania. The Eastburns adopted us. They had someone taking care of their children. In our disappointment they said, 'Oh come and hang out with us.' Our son played with their children. They gave Ron a jacket for the dining room, took us under their wing for meals and that first night, we went out bar hopping and danced and sang until four in the morning. We danced and sang all week and we've been going to the Chalfonte ever since.

"We could go to any hotel in the world but this one is unique. You can transport yourself to life in the 20s… to the 1890s. Mrs Satterfield was unique. She was a piece of work. She was a giant mama eagle. She sat at her family table making observations, would lower her head and say quietly, 'Oh, tacky.' I, too, needed to pass inspection. One summer I wore little dresses to the knee, made in Italy, silk and colorful in fuschia and orange. Meenie looked me up and down and said, 'Jule is that dress a mini?' Another day I came in with my hair in a bouffant, and Meenie said, 'Jule, is that your own hair?'

"Over the seasons our table grew, including the Gioni and Nowaki families, and we became more outrageous. One year Dick Sattler presented each with a gift: large red wax lips. We paraded in the dining room wearing large red wax lips for breakfast. The Chalfonte every August for us was one long laugh – a laugh for a week or two.

> **"We could go to any hotel in the world but this one is unique. You can transport yourself to life in the 20s… to the 1890s."**

"August was a busy time at the *SI* swimsuit edition. All the swimsuit shows are that time of year, and after the Chalfonte, I traveled on photo shoots for three months. The only phone is in a booth off the lobby. I set up shop in the booth for hours, calling swimsuit manufacturers and making resort reservations for models and the crew all over the world.

"We had a routine making our reservations at the Chalfonte. We stayed in the same room on the third floor with single beds [that's all there were – single beds] sagging like hammocks. I had back trouble so Ron would remind in advance that Theodore needed to put a door under my mattress. One August I stretch out and ouch! We investigate, and the door is knobside up." [Anne LeDuc has always maintained that the people vacationers meet are more important than the beds they sleep on.]

Ron Campbell "There weren't any locks on the doors, and you could leave your valuables, your jewelry in the safe in the lobby. I saw them open the safe one day and got curious, and went over later, and kicked lightly at the door, and it opened. No lock on the safe either.

"I had a friend, Hal Partenheimer, and he'd come for a week. And he did tricks about the Chalfonte inattention to detail. He checked in for his annual visit, and while in the lobby, turned the picture of the boat, the Lusitania, upside down. When he checked out a week later, the Lusitania was still upside down. He righted it on the way out the door.

"Hal's dearly departed and his name is on one of the rockers on the porch."

In a 1987 edition of the Chalfonte Newsletter, Ron discussed his love of the old hotel in a piece titled, 'What is the Chalfonte Experience?'

"I have spent better than 20 years trying to figure out just what the Chalfonte is and why it means so much to me. The difficulty lies in isolating single things, (i.e., the food, the people, the intrinsic beauty of the building, the memories) so that we tend to overlook the entire experience and the simple good feelings we always leave with more of. The Chalfonte becomes a corner of our lives that we would no more wish to do without than summer itself.

"There are other matters: we have friends of long standing we would not have had if it hadn't been for the Chalfonte. Obviously the same could be said of any place we had visited annually for 20 or more years, but I have to believe that the texture of these friendships is more finely woven, gentler and freer of obligation than others.

"And, like friendship, the Chalfonte survives change, is sometimes almost a symbol of change. This may be a funny thing to say about a hotel where dramatic alternations in the plumbing, furniture, menu and clientele tend to occur at glacial tempos, but it is important that they do take place, and aside from losing some of our most treasured friends over the years, most of

FAMILY TRADITION
For many seasons the Kendal Stackhouse family of Moorestown, New Jersey gathered at the Chalfonte for reunions, including four generations. Kendal is pictured, top center, in yellow shirt with glasses. Anne LeDuc, left, sitting on the railing, was always part of the fun. Anne and Kendal were childhood friends and later neighbors in Moorestown.
Photograph by Ben Luden

The Chalfonte

these changes are welcome.

"So, I guess the key word is friend. The Chalfonte cares and it's still there, still forgiving and always lovable… 6:30 at the Tin House, OK?"

* * *

The Court family has been vacationing at the Chalfonte for almost 100 years; their connection with the Satterfields dating back to Susie and Calvin Jr's reign starting in 1911. John Court was a toddler when he first enjoyed Chalfonte summers. He was the son of a naval officer, graduated from the Naval Academy in 1936, served in the Pacific Theater in World War II and Korea. He retired as a captain in 1959, graduated from William and Mary Law and practiced in Virginia and Maryland. His children, too, were Chalfonte regulars: Sally Court Rohrbach, Helen Glenn Court and sons Ken, Larry, John, Bill and Tony. Several worked at the hotel as have members of the third generation: Randy, Randolph, Mika,

PLAY TIME
John Court (holding the flag) with a friend at the hotel in 1921. John was one of the Chalfonte's best-known and best-loved regulars.
Court family collection

Brian, John, Christina, Courtenay, Than, Sarah, Elizabeth, BG and Ellyson.

John and Mimi Court were married for almost 63 years. Mimi passed away in 2005 and John died a year later. For many years, they vacationed annually at the Chalfonte with their children. In their later years, John and Mimi had a ritual of going twice a year, before the 4th of July and after Labor Day. John is remembered for his porch stories and Mimi for her mischievous humor.

The following is an excerpt from *Vignettes of a Felicitous Life* by John Martine Court…

"A very competent and faithful black girl whom I always knew as Bappy took over as my mentor, guardian, and retainer when I was first able to walk. We lived in the Lambert Street house [in Philadelphia] until well after the World War I ended. When Dad got orders to New York in 1920 I was four years old. Meanwhile, my parents had started spending the summers at the Chalfonte Hotel in Cape May, New Jersey, on the specific recommendations of Virginia friends in Norfolk. Dad, of course, could usually come down only on weekends, by train from Philadelphia or New York. Mother and Bappy and I had third floor rooms that I remember quite distinctly because of the ropes coiled in wooden troughs by each window. Fire regulations required these lifelines, but fortunately they were never needed.

"I also recall the great excitement of my going to the train station to meet Dad when he came down on weekends. There were two stations. The Reading stood at the center of town where the Acme parking lot is now (1990), and the Pennsylvania near the west end of the beach several blocks beyond Congress Hall. Horse-drawn station wagons took train passengers and their luggage from the station to their respective hotels. I got a big bang out of riding in the station wagons, particularly when I grew big enough to stand on the rear step and hold onto the vertical rails at the entrance to the passenger section.

"Among my friends and contemporaries were other Navy juniors whose parents were living in Philadelphia and sojourning for the summer at the Chalfonte, including Pret Haines, and Carolyn and Elaine Chantry, who have all predeceased me by a considerable margin. Some of our light amusements were sliding down the bannisters (to the great annoyance of Susie Satterfield, proprietress of the Chalfonte), attend-

FOREVER FRIENDS
The Satterfields and the Courts have been enjoying the Chalfonte together for more than 70 years.
Above: Anita Court and Calvin Satterfield Sr by the Chalfonte hydrangeas in 1921.
Court family collection

ing Punch and Judy shows in the hotel playroom, and clamoring for more desserts in the Children's Dining Room. You were supposed to be eight years old to eat in the main dining room.

"The most dramatic event, which I do not recall, but of which I was the central character, was so often retold by parents and the hotel hierarchy that it bears repeating. In the summer of 1917, while we were staying at the Chalfonte, I contracted such a severe case of croup that the local doctor arranged for a tracheotomy. As he was not qualified to perform the surgery and I was considered too ill to be taken to Philadelphia, Calvin Satterfield, son of the proprietress,

arranged to have a special train from Philadelphia bring the specialist, a Dr. McGlinn, who, as it turned out, owned a cottage at Cape May. This arrangement required a $200 cash deposit with the railroad. Dad did not have the amount with him, but another Chalfonte guest, Colonel Barbey, did and advanced it. In the end it turned out that a tracheotomy was unnecessary. I was revived by less strenuous treatment, considered a frail thing for years after, and fed much cod-liver oil (which, unless mixed with Scotch whisky, I found detestable) and beer (which I thoroughly enjoyed) and acidophilus milk (which I could have done without). Anyhow, I was always considered a rather puny child, and seemed to grow more slowly and be smaller than my contemporaries. Fortunately, however, I never broke any bones and had both a healthy appetite and plenty of energy, so my crisis in the summer of 1917 could not have been as dire as later described.

"After lunch one day Bappy led me up to the third floor for my nap. Some kind soul had given me a large yellow sourball to ease my anguish. Close to the top of the stairwell I stumbled and the sourball stuck in my throat. Bappy reacted instantaneously. She seized me by the ankles and held me over the banister upside down, giving me a violent jerk upward. The sourball flew out of my gaping mouth, heading toward the floor three flights down, where it hit and burst, to my great dismay and howling protest. Over 70 years later, I can still feel the shock of seeing that sourball depart.

"My parents owned a large Franklin touring car, which Mother undertook to drive down from Philadelphia to Cape May. She was a good driver and self-assured even though it was a dusty and bumpy four-hour drive over winding, country, dirt roads most of the way. A flat tire, however, was beyond the scope of her text. On one trip about 1920 we got a flat tire about 20 miles short of our destination. Mother flagged down the next car going our way. The occupants, who very politely stopped and proffered assistance, turned out to be ex-President William Howard Taft and chauffeur. I recall what a huge man Taft was and how graciously he offered us consolation while his chauffeur changed the tire and Mother apologized for her dusty condition. Taft became Chief Justice of the Supreme Court not long after and I was sure it was a fine appointment."

A FAMILIAR FACE
Above: John Court in his favorite perch on the Chalfonte porch in 1979.

Right: Gathering for Randolph Court's wedding at the hotel in 1999. Left to right: Randolph with his uncle Bill and father Joe.

Left: Chalfonte perennial Mimi Court, her husband John who summered at the hotel since he was a baby, and their grandson Than in 1982. Mimi seldom missed a summer vacation at the old hotel.

Court family collection

Sally Mead and Cricket Satterfield

Guest dress up for the "Meenie Awards"

Merrinelle Sullivan and Nancy Davey

Martha Nash and Sully Sullivan

Marge Strater, Martha Nash and Meenie Satterfield

Maria Satterfield, Harry Strater, Calvin "Sat" Satterfield III

Sandy Speer and Rosemary Mazon

Hotel staffers joining the party

Martha Nash

Nancy Davey and Eleanor Williams

Marge Strater in hat and Helen Dickerson

Sully Sullivan and Nancy Davey

Linda Riccio and Katie Kiliani Bliss

Calvin "Sat" Satterfield and Jule Campbell

Ron Campbell

Randolph Court and Jim Straw

Meenie Satterfield and Dick Bullington

Mimi Court and Diddy Mulligan

SAY CHEESE! Basking at the beach – a starring Chalfonte couple, Margaret and Jim Grove.

REMEMBERING
Above: Friends who have
passed are paid tribute
with their names in brass
plates on the porch rockers.
William D. "Bill" Lillard was a
Virginia gentleman who loved
bourbon, bridge and the
Beach Club in that order.

THE GOOD LIFE
Opposite: Sondy Sonderskov
and his wife Meredith enjoy
the porch breeze. They met
at the Chalfonte and return
every season. To their right:
Sondy's sister Mollibeth
(notorious for being able to
play the piano with her toes)
and her husband Fred Maley.
To the left of the photo: Jackie
Westervelt and Ed Baker.
Photos by John Lynner Peterson

CHAPTER VIII
The Soul Of
The Chalfonte

ELEN Dickerson, the famous Chalfonte cook, had as much to do with the hotel's survival as the owners. She spent virtually all of her 81 years in and about the kitchen. She was just a baby when Susie and Calvin Satterfield bought the Chalfonte. Her mother, Clementine Young, was the head chambermaid at the hotel and Helen always accompanied her mother. In winter, Clementine and Helen returned to Richmond, Virginia with the Satterfields and worked in their home.

When Helen was four she'd wait at the back alley door for Susie and together they would pick flowers for the dining tables. At age 12 Helen became a waitress, earning $3 a week. Then, too, she joined Susie in the gardens, collecting flowers for the lobby and dining room bouquets. A Helen habit was wearing one of the posies in her hair. She did so until her final days. Her favorites were roses.

Helen and Susie Satterfield were close. As Susie aged and arthritis caused her pain and anguish, Helen pushed her all over Cape May and Richmond in a high-backed wheelchair. They gossiped as they went and when the weather turned raw, Helen, at Susie's direction, would stop at the liquor store for a pint of bourbon. They each took sips and Susie stashed the bottle in one of the many pockets of her wheelchair. She felt the bourbon helped her arthritis.

Helen was tall, over five-foot-eight, statuesque and beautiful. And she was charismatic. There are those who say she could have been an actress; or, if she had been born half a century later, a TV anchor or politician. She could be funny as a stand-up comedian. Mostly, though, she is remembered for being a tough, but loving, manager and mother. She mothered more than just her blood children. Anne LeDuc called Helen her second mother, as did many Satterfields and dozens of young people who matured under her supervision in the kitchen. Daughter Lucille says that she and her sister Dot and step-sisters Cora and Joi never felt slighted. "We were well cared for," Lucille remembers. "We felt loved, no question about it, and Mama had a way about her of sharing herself with everyone. She was wise and gave good rules for the road. She lives in us still."

Helen worked her way up to head waitress and dining room manager. Her summer life

THE LADIES
Four generations from a legendary Chalfonte family: Left to right, Lucille Thompson; her sister Dot Burton; their mother, famous chef Helen Dickerson; and her mother, Clementine Young. Front: Dot's daughter, Tina, who still sometimes works at the hotel.
John Alexander collection

THE LADIES
Previous page: Dot and Lucille in the place they know best – the Chalfonte's famed kitchen.
Chalfonte collection

always revolved around the kitchen. She even slept near it – in a room steps from the kitchen door that she shared with her aunt Avis (Holmes). Her work day was long, from 6am to sometimes 10pm after a large and late dinner. She and her first husband, Fred Horsley, had two daughters – Dot in 1927 and Lucille in 1929. The little girls traveled with their mother and grandmother to the Chalfonte every season. "We went to school in Richmond," says Dot, "but in the fall when the hotel was being shut for the season, we sat in classes for two weeks or so in Cape May."

Helen was devoted to her work, the Chalfonte guests and the Satterfield family. Of all her gifts, devotion was probably the greatest. Nancy Satterfield Davey remembers when her grandmother Susie died in December, 1939,

the funeral in Richmond drew a large crowd. The church was full. And there, in full view, was Susie's empty wheelchair. It was a dramatic scene – the wheelchair placed there by Helen, her nurse, her devoted friend. (Fifty one years later, Helen would also die Christmas week.)

The 1940s were tough at the Chalfonte. Meenie Satterfield was a young widow with two sons on the battlefield in Europe and the South Pacific and a teenage daughter, Nancy, to raise. She was running the hotel by herself at a time of food and gas rationing. Helen stepped up to the challenge, becoming Meenie's partner in the dining room and kitchen. They planned the menus, ordered the food, went together to Alice's on Broadway for fresh produce and Schellinger's Landing for fish. They invented

BACK ALLEY
Chalfonte staff take a break. Front row, left to right: Alberta Price, Ren, unidentified, Theodore Roosevelt Jackson, Geraldine Brown, Charles Anderson, Dot Horsley (now Dot Burton). Back row: Cora Cook, Viva Toby, unidentified, Lucille Horsley (now Lucille Thompson), Elsie Walker.
Mead family collection

ways of using food ration stamps provided them by military guests. Winifred and Nora did the cooking while Helen observed and managed everything else. Around 1950, when Winifred no longer could carry on, Helen was asked to take over during a search for a chef. "And, they're still lookin'," she used to say.

Helen's daughters, in their 80s and still cooking at the Chalfonte, treasure diaries in the handwriting of their mother and Mrs Satterfield of menus, shopping lists, employee pay, weather and personal notes from the 1930s and 40s. Back then the main meal, or dinner, was served mid-day and a supper in the evening.

Luigi "Lou" Dickerson was a local – a large and dashing figure – who delivered ice to the hotel. He and Helen (who had divorced Fred

Wednesday, November 2

Kitchen Secrets

Excerpts from the Chalfonte's kitchen diary from the 1930s and 40s.

Thursday, July 23, 1936
No Mosquitoes! Beautiful Day.
Sea Breeze.
BREAKFAST
Sliced Peaches
Eggs – Bacon – Fish
DINNER
Roast Lamb
Potatoes – Corn
Huckleberry Roll – Vanilla Ice Cream
SUPPER
Chicken Hash – Grits
Tomato Salad
Strawberry Jam
5 legs – 2 rolls (1 leg too much)
Number Fed 94

Tuesday, August 13, 1940
Beautiful Day!
BREAKFAST
Canteloupe
Liver & Bacon
DINNER
Roast Beef
Potatoes – Corn – Limas –Beets
Pie & Vanilla Ice Cream
SUPPER
Chicken Croquettes
Tomato Salad
Bartlett Pears
(6 rib roast 1-7 lb chuck)
Number Fed 117

Monday, Labor Day, 1940
BREAKFAST
Tomato Juice
Ham & Eggs
DINNER
Roast Lamb
Snaps – Squash – Corn – Potatoes
Vanilla Fudge Ice Cream & Rice Pudding
SUPPER
Hamburgers
French Fries
Tomato Salad
Peaches
Number Fed 105

WORDS OF WISDOM
Handed down by their mother Helen Dickerson, the diaries were treasured by Chalfonte cooks Dot Burton and Lucille Thompson – they detailed menus for three meals a day, shopping lists, and notes on the hours worked by staff.

KITCHEN STAFF
**Front, left to right, Tina Bowser, her mother Dot Burton, Dot's sister Lucille Thompson.
Second row, left to right, Calvin Matterson, Helen Dickerson, unidentified, Charles
Thompson. Back row, Frezel Burton, Dot's husband, and Dot's son, Jimmy Burton.**
Mead family collection

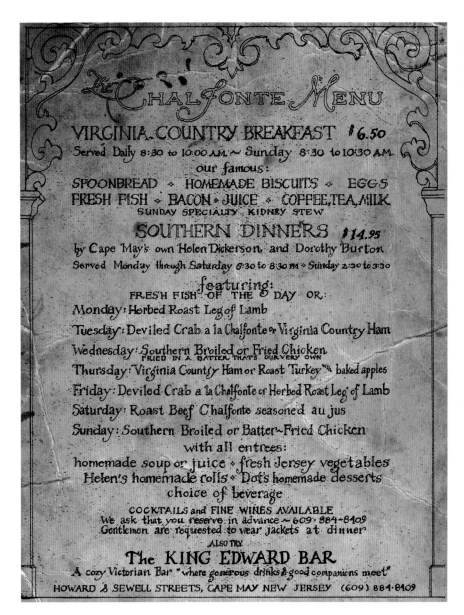

The CHALFONTE MENU

VIRGINIA COUNTRY BREAKFAST $6.50
Served Daily 8:30 to 10:00 A.M. ~ Sunday 8:30 to 10:30 A.M.
our famous:
SPOONBREAD ◇ HOMEMADE BISCUITS ◇ EGGS
FRESH FISH ◇ BACON ◇ JUICE ◇ COFFEE, TEA, MILK
SUNDAY SPECIALTY · KIDNEY STEW

SOUTHERN DINNERS $14.95
by Cape May's own Helen Dickerson and Dorothy Burton
Served Monday through Saturday 6:30 to 8:30 PM ~ Sunday 2:30 to 3:30
featuring:
FRESH FISH OF THE DAY OR:
Monday: Herbed Roast Leg of Lamb
Tuesday: Deviled Crab a la Chalfonte or Virginia Country Ham
Wednesday: Southern Broiled or Fried Chicken
FRIED IN A BATTER THAT'S OUR VERY OWN
Thursday: Virginia Country Ham or Roast Turkey with baked apples
Friday: Deviled Crab a la Chalfonte or Herbed Roast Leg of Lamb
Saturday: Roast Beef Chalfonte seasoned au jus
Sunday: Southern Broiled or Batter-Fried Chicken
with all entrees:
homemade soup or juice ◇ fresh Jersey vegetables
Helen's homemade rolls ◇ Dot's homemade desserts
choice of beverage
COCKTAILS and FINE WINES AVAILABLE
We ask that you reserve in advance ~ 609·884·8409
Gentlemen are requested to wear jackets at dinner
ALSO TRY
The KING EDWARD BAR
A cozy Victorian Bar "where generous drinks & good companions meet"
HOWARD & SEWELL STREETS, CAPE MAY NEW JERSEY (609) 884·8409

Horsley more than 10 years earlier) met during the deliveries, fell in love and were married in 1950. The Cape May-Richmond migration ended for Helen. She and Luigi settled down in a little house on Sunset Boulevard with Lou's chickens out back.

Helen's duties were onerous. She routinely cooked for 120 guests, and for years, there were three meals a day. Breakfasts featured spoon bread, eggs and bacon and/or ham, a fried fish (usually weak fish), hot biscuits, green fried tomatoes in season on Fridays and kidney stew on Sundays. The dinner menus, always with homemade yeast rolls, were repeated weekly: roast lamb on Monday, roast beef on Tuesday, fried chicken on Wednesday, country ham or turkey on Thursday, crab croquettes and broiled bluefish on Friday. Some specials included scal-

CLASSIC DISHES
A Chalfonte menu showing the downhome Southern selections that made the hotel famous.
Chalfonte collection

lops and mushrooms mornay, Lucille's corn pudding, eggplant casserole. There was always a major Sunday dinner with all the fixings at mid-day. Dinners featured a juice or soup and a heavy dessert: seasonal fruit pies, cobblers, Helen's apple and pound cakes, Dot's Lemon Meringue Pie. The staff worked seven days a week, getting off only at 2:30pm on Sunday afternoons. On Sunday evenings, Theodore's beach picnics at Higbee's Beach with large lob-

THREE OF A KIND
Lucille Thompson, her mother Helen Dickerson and sister Dot Burton in their kitchen whites. Like their mother, the sisters are still working in the kitchen, even in their 80s.
Photograph by Judy Bartella

sters became legendary.

Before chefs became celebrities on Food Network and morning network shows, Helen already had been discovered by television producers. She appeared on the *Phil Donahue Show, Lifestyles with Regis Philbin, The Sally Jessy Raphael Show* and numerous other TV and radio shows, sharing her recipes for some of her specialties: fried chicken, spoon bread and collards. It is obvious, from looking at the old menus and considering Helen's recipes, that she definitely added her own tastes, flavors and dishes to the Chalfonte menu. She's called a cook, but she had chef skills.

Helen was a woman of remarkable energy. Dressed in her kitchen white, often with a colorful handkerchief in her pocket, she would leave her kitchen post and move about the dining room, welcoming perennial guests who considered her family. As she aged and her pace

slowed, the guests would come to the kitchen for some Helen affection and gift her with flowers or bourbon.

Especially in the off-season, she gave freely of her culinary skills to her community, preparing church suppers with the same love- in- the-pot she gave as chef at the Chalfonte. In high season, she packed up hotel leftovers and delivered to the neighborhood needy. Asked what is it that made her so special, her daughter Lucille says, "She was just born that way. The Chalfonte was her home, always. She grew up at the hotel, lived there, and she treated it with the love and respect you treat your house and your family."

"She always said she wanted to die with her boots on right here in the kitchen," said daughter Dot. "She worked here until a month before she died. This will always be her kitchen. It is here in the kitchen that we still feel her spirit watching over us as we make her dinner rolls, crab cakes and fried chicken."

Just as Satterfield family descendants in a fourth and fifth generation continue to work at the hotel, Helen Dickerson's descendants do so as well. Dot's daughters Tina and Lynnette continue the tradition working in 2010 with their mother, 83, and aunt Lucille, 81, who vow to retire every season, only to return the next year frying the chicken, rolling the crab cakes and pinching the yeast rolls.

The following article, "The Ladies", written by Karen Fox, originally appeared in Cape May Magazine *in August, 2009:*

There are few historic hostelries in this

BEAN PICKIN'
Above: The kitchen staff select and trim fresh green beans for dinner in the alley. In the background are Diddy Mulligan and Dot Burton.
Chalfonte collection

Top: A menu for a dinner to celebrate Cape May's National Historic Landmark status.

world where the eras of architecture and food embrace each other. At the Chalfonte, Cape May's oldest continuous hotel, the Magnolia Room's southern menu has been a tradition for 98 years. That is remarkable in itself. But more remarkable, the dishes: the fried chicken, split pea soup, herbed roast leg of lamb, baked ham, black-eyed peas, crab croquettes, fried eggplant, collards and ham hocks, fried green tomatoes, spoon bread, corn pudding, butter milk biscuits,

sweet potato pie, blueberry cobbler, have been lovingly produced by three generations of women from one Virginia family. In all, they have given more than 200 years of themselves at the Chalfonte.

In summer, the long, lacey scalloped verandas provide the same cool shade for rocking as they did the year Civil War hero Colonel Henry Sawyer built the Chalfonte in 1876.

The dining room is elegant in its unspoiled plainness. Ocean breezes float from tall windows, refreshing as they were the evening Mr. Sawyer sat down for his first dinner. The heart of the hotel is, and always has been, the kitchen. The big black coal-burning stoves are gone and the giant iceboxes are no more. But the family of cooks that has made this kitchen nationally famous still reigns this summer of 2008. They describe their distinctive style as 'soul food with its Sunday clothes on.'

TEAM EFFORT
Above: The Chalfonte's kitchen staff prepare for one of the hotel's popular Victorian dinners.
Photograph by Judy Bartella

MAN AT WORK
Right: Dot's husband, known only as Burton, often peeled several boxes of potatoes in an afternoon. He also was the person who cleaned the kidneys for the Satterfield's favorite Sunday breakfast item, kidney stew.
Photograph by Judy Bartella

PURSGLOVE 2, THE BUTCHER 3, TV/RADIO 7-10, MOVIES 11-12, CROSSWORD 14, BRIDGE/DEAR ABBY/CHESS 15

Magazine

ACCENT ON FOOD

THE CHALFONTE:
SOUTHERN COOKING
AT THE SHORE

By Cissy Finley Grant, P.4

CHEF HELEN DICKERSON (RIGHT) AND DAUGHTER DOT BURTON IN FRONT OF THE CHALFONTE, CAPE MAY, N.J.   PHOTO BY JULIA GAINES/THE WASHINGTON TIMES

Their fried chicken is the Chalfonte special that has attracted the most attention from food writers and national TV shows over the years. And it is beyond a doubt the most popular among guests. The chicken is deep golden crispy crunchy on the outside, moist on the inside, with a pungent scent and flavor all its own.

The Chalfonte food is essentially southern home cooking, using locally grown ingredients with recipes capable of serving 150 to 200. It is the home cookin' that helps make the old hotel feel like home for the guests who return year after year, from one generation to the next, to rooms that have had no air conditioning, televisions, internet, and only shared baths. It is one of the only hotel kitchens anywhere where guests burst in for hellos, hugs, kisses and gifts of flowers and scotch for the cooks who are considered family.

Imagine a splendid day in early October,

late in the afternoon. Shafts of strong sunlight beam across the cavernous kitchen throwing prisms off shiny pots. 'The Ladies' – Dot Burton and Lucille Thompson, sisters, 81 and 79 – move about in a slow sashay, preparing for the last meal of the season. They claim this will be their 'last supper.' They have worked the Chalfonte their entire lives. They are weary, looking forward to winter, retirement, their own rocking chairs and watching soap operas without interruption.

The nostalgia in the kitchen this 'last supper' is palpable, but there are no tears. There is joy in the routine of what the sisters do so well, putting their hearts and souls into their food preparations. Lucille is rolling crab croquettes to the size of little loaves of bread and dipping them in egg and spiced bread crumbs. There is the rhythm of experience in her hands.

Dot reaches up to the rack holding uten-

FRYING CHICKEN
Above: Lucille and Dot in their element as kitchen manager Chris Cleary learns some secrets of the Magnolia Room's famous fried chicken.
Watercolor by Marie Natale

STAR ATTRACTIONS
Opposite, clockwise from top left: Dot and her mother Helen featured in *The Washington Times* in 1984; Helen was on the *Phil Donahue Show* in 1984; Dot and Lucille with The Food Network's Tyler Florence, who traveled to the Chalfonte in 2003 in his nationwide search for the best fried chicken – and found it.
Judy Bartella collection
Nancy Granick

sils, pots and pans and grabs one of the heavy black cast iron skillets. It is two feet wide with a three-foot handle that easily holds a dozen or so chicken quarters. "This big old thing is about 100 years old and that is older than me," says Dot with a chuckle. "How many pieces of chicken has this pan fried? Only the Lord knows."

Dot was nine years old when she started here 73 years ago. Lucille was seven. Their first job was to rinse sand from guests' bathing suits. Once finished, they hung the suits on the door knobs of the rooms. There was the time when the sisters got in a fight and engaged in a tug-of-war with a suit. It spit in half, and they had to forfeit their wages to buy a new one. "That's the way life lessons were taught back then," says Dot.

Lucille bends beneath a long stainless steel table and hoists to the top yeast rolls that have been rising under snow white towels. "This is

our mother Helen Dickerson's famous hot rolls recipe," says Lucille. "I make 12 dozen most days, and have added my own touches. In a hurry one day to cool the yeast mix, I added some ice cream. The vanilla flavor was special, and ever since I add ice cream to every batch."

Ice cream. The very mention of ice cream reminds Lucille – Ceilly – of a favorite memory. "Come with me," she says, leading the way out the kitchen, across the alley, to a white box of a small building. "The Coal Bin," she announces. "When we were girls, our grandmother Clementine, my sister Dot and I slept on iron beds in the same room as the coal. Later on, they added this bedroom with windows. At night, we'd wait until Clementine was snoring loud as thunder. We'd sneak out the bed, crawl out the window, and run down town to see what was goin' on. Clementine loved ice cream. It was our ticket back to bed! We bribed her with ice cream, and Grandma, don't you dare tell Mama we were AWOL. Mama was a disciplinarian."

Helen Dickerson ruled the Chalfonte kitchen for 45 years with a tough hand, lusty humor and

From The Archives

▌ Excerpt from The Chalfonte Newsletter, 1989: A Conversation with Helen Dickerson...

Why have you worked all these years at the Chalfonte? It was my home. I felt like I had a brick, a piece of the hotel.

We hear you're having a birthday! I'll be 80 and I've been retiring ever since I was 60, but they ain't gonna get rid of me because I am going to sit right here with my boots on.

Do you feel like a celebrity? To be put up in a hotel in Chicago [for the *Phil Donahue Show* in 1984] and have wine, a linen table cloth and room service? If that is heaven, then let me go.

What are some of the changes at the hotel? My salary. My first pay was $3 a week.

a warm heart. "Mother was in her starched kitchen whites, ready to go to work, at 6:30 every morning. She'd be waiting at the back door to welcome the help," says Dot. "She expected a 'Good Mornin' from every one. If any one had the head down, a hangover, an attitude, Mama said real loud, 'Well, good mornin. Did I sleep with you last night?' That broke it up, whatever it was."

Once when a cook chain-smoked, against Chalfonte rules, Helen waited for the propitious moment, threw a piece of wadded-up dough and hit him smack in the forehead. "He never ever smoked in the kitchen again," says Dot.

There was the calamity when a disgruntled cook threw a big pot at a dishwasher. The pot sideswiped the dishwasher and hit the wall hard, suffering a big dent. Miss Helen strode over, picked up the pot, handed it to the cook to wash, and put it back in service. She eyed all the help eyeing her, and never saying a word, went back to work. So did everyone else. "There's the pot," says Lucille. "It's still in use and it always reminds us of Mama."

Helen Dickerson was a fixture at the Chalfonte for 77 years. She came to the hotel as a child with mother, Clementine Young, who worked winters for the owners, the Satterfield family, in Richmond, Virginia, and summers, at the Chalfonte. Helen was four when she first set foot in the kitchen, sitting in a little chair at the back door, waiting to join Miss Susie Satterfield, picking flowers for the dining room tables. Helen's mother Clementine was hard at work on the second floor making beds and cleaning rooms. Clementine began chambermaid duties at age 12, and worked those same rooms, pleasing guests for 60 years. "She was a portrait in service and loyalty," says granddaughter Lucille. "Our mother Helen showed the same devotion to duty in the kitchen.

When times get hot in the kitchen on sultry summer days, with competing egos, dinner deadlines and yet more chicken to fry, a cooling-off spot is the Tin House, especially in June and July when the pink roses entwine the fence and the lattice, perfuming the air. The Tin House is an overgrown dollhouse about 12 by 22 feet, hidden from the street by a tall hedge. If you don't know the white and green structure is there, you could pass it by for years.

The Tin House was born of desperation. "There was a Philadelphia man who could not pay Calvin Satterfield his hotel bill," says Anne LeDuc, who with Judy Bartella, owned, restored and operated the Chalfonte for 25 years until late summer, 2008. The delinquent guest shipped tin cutouts to Mr Satterfield for payment, and the result is the charming little building. "It was where they hid the bourbon and whiskey in Prohibition," says Anne, who has summered at the Chalfonte since age two. She remembers the pomp of the place when the wait staff shined their tables' silver to gleaming perfection. They carried little cotton towels to polish goblets before meals. The white-gloved maitre d', William, seated the guests in their dinner attire. The wait staff stood against the wall, hands behind their backs until ready to spring into polite action, serving the plates.

Like the Satterfields, Anne is from a Virginia family. "The Virginians and West Virginians loved their bourbon," says Anne, "and that included the women. I was astonished at their capacity. I looked in the window of the Tin House one day, and there was Mother at a party, hanging from her knees from a beam. The Tin House parties are legendary. Guests gave their

TOOL OF THE TRADE
Dot with one of the Chalfonte's legendary pans.

KIDDIE DINING
Opposite: Susie Satterfield started the tradition of the Children's Dining Room almost a century ago. It was a big benefit for the parents who could eat dinner in peace.

own cocktail parties at the Tin House before we had the King Edward Bar. They ordered their favorite hors d'oeuvres. Helen and the kitchen provided them. Most popular were the miniature warm biscuits sandwiching Virginia ham spread.

"To this day, the Tin House and the Wedding Tree, the big lovely willow, are favorite spots for parties and nuptials," says Anne. "And the shenanigans continue. One morning I went out to smell the roses, and a couple was having a Magnolia Room breakfast on the roof. They had hoisted the little patio table and two chairs to the roof – to get a view of the ocean, perhaps.

"Various of our staff have preferred living in the Tin House with its bed, bureau and chair," says Anne. "We have had some characters." Anne recalls handyman extraordinaire, Theodore, whose car was the love of his life. "Theodore could not drive," says Anne. "But he required the benefit of a garage for his beloved sedan. Once or twice a summer, his friend would come up from Richmond, and with great ceremony, drive the two of them around town. Theodore could do anything. Fix leaky pipes with gauze. Stoke the coal fires. Carve the meat. I still miss Theodore." Anne mists over remembering. "They say I should write a book."

In the early days of the LeDuc-Bartella regime at the Chalfonte, one of the staff did write a book, a precious tome chronicling the recipes the Virginia ladies cooked by instinct: their touch, taste and feel. The cookbook is called *I Just Quit Stirrin' When the Tastin's Good*, quoting Helen Dickerson as she struggled to explain her recipes and methods. She was prodded on by Cissy Finley Grant, who dutifully wrote down the measurements, not for the usual 150 – 200 meals Helen was accustomed to turning out, but for servings from six to 12. Cissy's brother-in-law, Bill Grant, told her it was a project, "like putting folklore in your stomach." The project consumed the cooks, Helen, Dot and Lucille, through the summer of 1985 – testing, retesting and testing again the recipes.

The result is a 94-page cookbook, still available in the lobby, that has gone home with thousands of Cape May visitors. The recipes represent combined cultures. There are the flavors of the European cuisine that graced the tables of the Virginia aristocracy on plantations robust with game, garden vegetables and orchard fruits. Through the years, African-American cooks added the tastes and textures from their slave cabin kitchens to the main house menus. From one generation to the next, the foods melded into the good ol' southern cooking still served today at the Chalfonte's Magnolia Room.

Back in the kitchen, Dot is standing over the two big old cast-iron skillets, bubbling with oil, and mounds of sliced onions. She swirls around the onions, allowing them to crisp before adding the chicken quarters that have been soaking in a salt brine. "The onions are our secret," says Dot.

From The Archives

A letter from Anne LeDuc on January, 1991...

Dear Friends

Please forgive the impersonal greeting, but I have the sad task of notifying you and many others of Helen Dickerson's passing on December 23, 1990. The blessing is she "died with her boots on," just as she had wanted, having worked until the first week In November... The Memorial service, at the Macedonian Baptist Church on December 24, was indeed a celebration of life. Reverend Davis was wonderful, captured the essence of Helen, playing "The Saints Go Marching In", and other songs. Hope to see you in '91. Anne LeDuc

Quotes from Anne LeDuc, December, 1990...

"I've been on the phone for 12 hours. The outpouring of affection is unbelievable. She was very popular with guests and had a wonderful rapport with the staff... It's the end of an era. We miss terribly a person who's been involved in a family-like situation and who's been a vital part of the operation of the hotel. But mostly we miss the person herself – her brightness, kindness, leadership, gentility and wit. The way she used to slap your fingers with a fly swatter because you took something she was working on.

"We will celebrate her life. A lot of Helen will go with each one of us in different ways."

"The onions and the paprika in the flour that helps turn the chicken golden brown." The smell of the onions frying sends the olfactory and saliva glands into mouthwatering anticipation.

Dot dredges the chicken pieces in the flour, salt, pepper and paprika mixture, coating each piece, and drops them in the bubbling oil. She never leaves her station during the 20 to 30 minutes it takes for each panful to cook and crisp. Then she lays the pieces on a rack over a baking pan to drip off any oil, and places it in a warming oven until it is time to plate and serve Dot's Famous Fried Chicken in the Magnolia Room.

Late last summer Anne LeDuc and Judy Bartella sold the Chalfonte to Bob and Linda Mullock. Anne winces at the emotional pain, but the Mullocks are determined to maintain the historical ambiance of the place. "And, they'll keep the Tin House," says Anne. "That was always a barometer to me – of trust – to keep it the way it is, with some updated amenities, like bathrooms and air conditioning."

And 'The Ladies'? They are back! No rocking chairs on cool verandas for them this season. New owner Bob Mullock says, "The Ladies cannot NOT come back. They are the heart and soul of the place. I cannot imagine life here without them," he says. "How would I survive without their fried chicken?"

Mullock was married at the hotel in 1981 when he and his wife, Linda, were in the first year of running a B&B they restored called the Victorian Rose, just a few steps from the Chalfonte. One of Mullock's favorite photos is a picture of him and his bride in their wedding regalia in the kitchen with 'The Ladies'. And that evening, Bob remembers fetching Helen from the kitchen and dancing with her. (See Chapter 12.)

The Chalfonte is that way. She gets into your soul and then you are beholden to her.

ALFRESCO DINING
Opposite: The Magnolia Room offers dining on the Sewell Avenue porch. Guests enjoy ocean breezes and hear the clip-clop of horse-drawn carriages on historic street tours.
Cape May Publishing

KITCHEN TABLE
Following page: Much of life at the Chalfonte evolves around the kitchen table. The Ladies make time for generations of family and friends and that's part of the charm of the place. Brenda Bartella Peterson pays a visit.
Photograph by John Lynner Peterson

GOOD MORNIN'
Helen Dickerson, early in her dining
room- kitchen career in the 40s.
She was always at work by 6:30 and
insisted on a proper "good mornin'"
from her staff. And opposite, Helen
toward the end of more than 70 years
at the Chalfonte. She started as a
child and was chef for almost half a
century, working until she was 81.
Chalfonte collection
Opposite, by Dennis McDonald

From The Archives

▒ Obituary from *The Philadelphia Inquirer*, December 31, 1990.

HELEN DICKERSON
1909 – 1990

Helen Dickerson was famous for her eggplant casserole and crab cakes. But visitors to the Chalfonte Hotel also remember her unbridled wit and outspokenness.

Mrs Dickerson, 81, who worked for the Chalfonte Hotel for 70 years, died Friday, December 21, 1990. In her time, she became one of the hotel's most beloved figures. A woman known for her generosity and warmth.

Excerpt from The Chalfonte Newsletter 1991:

"I like to imagine Miss Helen in God's largest rose garden directing the pruners." – Emily Green, Lansdale, Pennsylvania

"To me Helen was, and always will be, a woman of great wisdom and dedication, who was greater than life, but always humble. She showed me that patience, love and respect will provide a person with more in life than anything else." – Rob Sumner, Baltimore, Maryland

"Her warmth and welcoming spirit will forever greet me in Cape May – each time I enter the hotel." – Katie Kiliani Bliss, Maplewood, New Jersey

"I thought about the first summer, 20 years ago when I met Helen. It started out with absolute fear... to a crazy love and admiration. She always claimed to have eyes in the back of her head, and I never doubted it for a moment. Helen was a combination of cook, mother, confidante, Ann Landers, teacher, comedian, monarch and the life of the party." – Susan Hunsiker Howard, Dedham, Massachusetts.

A Special Taste Of The Chalfonte

The following recipes were excerpted from the cookbook *I Quit Stirrin' When the Tastin's Good*, published in 1986 and edited by Cissy Finley Grant, former Chalfonte Public Relations Director.

"I Just Quit Stirrin' When The Tastin's Good"

SWEET POTATO PIE
4 medium sweet potatoes
2 eggs
½ cup sugar
1 teaspoon vanilla
½ teaspoon ground nutmeg
Pinch salt
½ pound butter
½ cup evaporated milk
1 unbaked prepared pie shell

Boil potatoes until soft. Peel and place in mixing bowl. Beat until there are no lumps. Add remaining ingredients. Beat until creamy. Pour into a prepared pie shell and bake at 350 degrees until knife inserted in the center comes out clean – approximately 1 hour and 10 minutes. If crust edges brown too quickly, cover edges with thin strip of foil.

CHALFONTE BUTTERMILK BISCUITS
Mix: 2 cups all-purpose flour, 2 teaspoons baking power, ½ teaspoon salt, pinch sugar.
Blend: 4 tablespoons Crisco into dry mixture, until well blended. (Lucille mixes by hand.)
Add: Gradually 3/4 cup buttermilk until dough is manageable. Do not mix until too sticky.
Roll: On floured board until dough is 3/4-inch thick. Cut out biscuits, about the size of a silver dollar.
Bake: On greased pan (Pam) at 400 degrees until brown on top, around 20 minutes.
For decoration, Lucille tapes three forks together and gently prods each biscuit.

SPLIT PEA SOUP
1 ham hock
1 pound bag split peas
1 quart chicken stock
1 medium onion, chopped
2 bay leaves
1 potato, diced
1 carrot, diced
Salt and pepper to tate

Soak peas overnight. Drain. Cook ham hock about 1 ½ hours in 2 quarts water. Combine hock, water and remaining ingredients, and simmer until peas are soft, or 2 to 3 hours. Press through sieve or strainer. Will thicken after it sits a while. Yield: 3 quarts.

BAKED STUFFED TOMATOES
Prepare: 8 large round, firm tomatoes. Wash and core. Scoop out enough in middle to allow for stuffing. Place in Pyrex baking dish. Add 1 teaspoon melted bacon fat to each tomato. Sprinkle with salt, pepper and ½ teaspoon sugar.
Mince: 1 medium onion and 1 large green pepper.
Stuff: Tomatoes with minced vegetables
Sprinkle: Breadcrumbs on top of each tomato. Cover dish with foil. Bake at 350 degrees approximately 45 minutes or until tomatoes are tender.
Serves 8

CRAB CROQUETTES
1 pound back fin crab meat, picked
2 tablespoons fresh parsley
2 tablespoons grated onion
1 tablespoon fresh lemon juice
1 cup thick cream sauce
1 egg
1 teaspoon Worcestershire sauce
1/8 teaspoon pepper
2 drops Tabasco, optional

Mix, with hands carefully, but do not overwork, the crab meat and all other ingredients listed above. Shape into croquetes. Roll each croquette in the following mixture.

1 cup crushed breadcrumbs
1 teaspoon paprika
2 eggs

Let sit for about an hour before frying. Fry in deep fat at 375 degrees until brown, 4 to 5 minutes.
Serves 6

DOT'S HAM SPREAD
Mix: 3/4 pound country ham, ground, with enough Hellman's mayonnaise (if you don't make your own) to make it spreadable. Spread on split biscuits and heat in oven until hot. Great for hors d'oeuvres – as served at Tin House parties.

SPOON BREAD
1 cup Indian Head white corn meal
3 eggs, well beaten
3 cups milk
2 tablespoons butter
1 ½ teaspoons salt
3 teaspoons baking powder

Preheat oven to 450 degrees. Combine butter, corn meal and 2 cups of milk in pan, cooking slowly over medium heat. Bring mixture just to a boil, stirring constantly. Blend eggs, salt and remaining milk. Add to the corn meal mixture. Mix well. Stir in the baking powder. Pour into greased 1 ½ to 2-quart casserole. Bake 25-35 minutes. Serve hot, with butter. Serves 6-8.

HELEN'S THICK CREAM SAUCE
3 tablespoons butter
½ cup flour
1 cup milk or light cream, heated
Salt
Freshly ground pepper

Melt butter in heavy-bottomed saucepan. Stir in flour and cook, stirring constantly, until the paste cooks and bubbles a bit, but don't let it brown – about two minutes. Add hot milk or cream, continuing to stir as the sauce thickens. Bring to a boil. Add salt and pepper to taste. Lower the heat and cook, stirring, for 2-3 minutes more until thick. Remove from heat. You may cool this sauce for later use; in that case, cover it with wax paper or pour a film of milk over it to prevent skin from forming.
Yield: 1 cup

POTS 'N' PANS A work of art in in their age and use, some of this kitchen equipment has been cooking for decades. John Lynner Peterson

CHALFONTE'S SOUTHERN FRIED CHICKEN

1 frying chicken (3 pound) quartered
Salt
1 cup flour
2 tablespoons paprika
Black pepper to taste
2 cups shortening or corn oil (or a 2-inch depth for frying)
1 medium onion, sliced

1: Soak the chicken in salted water for 1 hour. (Add 1 tablespoon salt to each quart of water.) Drain chicken and pat dry.
2: Meanwhile, in a bag or bowl, mix flour, paprika, salt to taste and pepper. Add the chicken and shake to coat thoroughly.
3: In a large skillet or deep fryer, heat the shortening or oil to 365 to 375 degrees. Place the onion in the hot oil. (Adjust the heat as needed to keep the oil sizzling moderately, but don't let it burn.)
4: Add the chicken to hot oil, again adjusting the heat. Fry for 10 minutes.

Turn chicken and fry until tender, crisp and browned, about 10 more minutes. (Test for doneness with a fork, or watch for the breast meat to split along the muscle.)
Note: As long as the oil is sizzling, moisture is being forced out of the chicken as steam, preventing the meat from absorbing excess oil.

Dot places the fried chicken on a rack over a baking pan, and keeps the chicken warm in the oven until served.

CHAPTER IX
Rogues, Entrepreneurs & Adventurers

"HELLO, Chalfonte Hotel. This is Maria." The embracing voice on the reservation phone the summer of 2010 belonged to a fifth generation of Satterfields to work at the old hotel. Maria Neligan is the great-great granddaughter of Susie Satterfield, who instilled her brand of southern living at the hotel 100 years ago. Maria has been summering in and around the hotel since she was a baby in a stroller at Franklin Street Cottage, accompanied by her brothers Boone and Jack. Maria's mother Susan (Susie) is named for her great-grandmother.

Susan "Susie" Satterfield Neligan *Charlottesville, Virginia* "I started working at the hotel as a young girl – 15 – in the Children's Dining Room. Then I worked the front desk, and my friend and I were the first barmaids when the King Eddie opened. For me the hotel is overwhelmingly emotional at times, a sacred space, feeling the spirit of my family before me – Meenie, my grandmother whom we called Vovo, my father Sat. I wanted to stay near here, and in 1993, my sister Mary Minor [named for Meenie] Taylor and I bought the house just across the street, the yellow house, so that we can socialize and have meals here. Soon after, my sister bought the house behind the yellow bungalow. Our backyards join. My sister Alice Tor rents a house nearby for her family. And my brother Calvin IV, his family, including son Calvin V, visit each summer."

Susie remembers a historic moment and shows the alley and balcony where it happened. She was a child, swinging in the back, when on July 28, 1966, about 20 of the African-American staff, mostly college students, gathered in the alley in protest. Meenie Satterfield heard noises. She walked from her room to a second floor balcony overlooking the alley. The staff was vocal in demanding a pay raise. Meenie gathered herself on the balcony and addressed the group, saying that a pay raise was impossible, that she could not afford to pay more. The protestors were emphatic; then threatened to walk off the job. In that case, Meenie said, they would have to go. Waiters, kitchen helpers, chambermaids left. It was the middle of summer. The hotel was full. Susie remembers there was chaos, but guests and families pitched in to get meals on the table, and rooms tidied. Guest at the time, Ron Campbell, recalls that two of the students,

GENERATIONS
Maria Neligan and a portrait of her great-grandmother Meenie Satterfield in the lobby of the Chalfonte. Maria has vacationed at the hotel since she was a child and joined the long line of Satterfields working summers at the hotel.
Photo by Dale Gerhard, courtesy of *Press of Atlantic City*

BELOVED
The Chalfonte's legendary handyman, Theodore Roosevelt Jackson.
Photo by Judy Bartella

a brother and sister, stayed on. They had called their mother in tears. Their mother said they had made a contract with Mrs Satterfield for a certain pay for certain work, and they needed to fulfill their commitment.

The civil rights movement was at its peak at the time. Stokely Carmichael gave his black power speech on that same day, July 28, 1966. Dr Martin Luther King was preparing to take the civil rights movement north to Chicago. Marches in Alabama the year before led to Congress passing the Voting Rights Act. African-Americans began going to polls in greater numbers in 1966 and making a difference in elections. But for the most part, harmony reigned among the hotel's large African-American staffers during

those years of turmoil.

There has been a parade of characters staffing the Chalfonte over the years worthy of a Broadway musical. Among the most memorable: chambermaid Clementine Young, daughter Helen Dickerson, the nationally famous southern cook, housekeeper Martha Nash, head housekeeper and hostess Diddy Christian-Mulligan, handyman Theodore Roosevelt Jackson, bellman Henry Thatch, maitre d' William Waller, iceman Luigi Dickerson. They were hard working, dedicated, and gave large parts of their lives to making the Chalfonte hotel a unique vacation experience. Many staffers were members of the Satterfield family. Their services have spanned a century.

Cricket Satterfield *Richmond, Virginia* "I spent a lot of time around the kitchen, trying to catch a ride with Helen the cook's husband, Luigi Dickerson, the iceman. He wore a big brown leather cape, and hauled massive blocks of ice on his back – 350 pounds of ice! He was the strongest man I have ever known. There was no refrigerator in the hotel. I'd watch him deliver the ice at the Chalfonte, and whenever I could, I'd ride around town on the back of his ice truck in the 50s.

HANDYMAN EXPERTISE
This page, left: Theodore Roosevelt Jackson was a man known for being able to fix anything. Some of his wrappings on plumbing pipes just recently were removed.

JOIE DE VIVRE
Right: Cora is remembered for having a great sense of humor no matter the chore. She worked at the hotel in the 40s.

LIFE'S SERVICE
Opposite, far left: Clementine Young spent 60 years as a chambermaid. In winters she worked for the Satterfield family in Richmond.

ALLEY TIME
Opposite: The staff gathered in the alley between the kitchen and the building in the background called The Quarters. It served as the coal bin and bedrooms for Clementine, second from left, and for her granddaughters Dot and Lucille.

THE BELLMAN
Opposite, below: Ernest "Boots" Mead conversing with Henry "Bunches" Thatch, the bellman who prided himself in being able to answer all questions about the Chalfonte and Cape May. Or as one guest put it, "Henry was pre-Google."
Mead family collection

"Luigi the iceman planted the willow tree in the back yard of the Chalfonte, behind the Tin House, scene of many parties and weddings over the years. That tree is 60 years old and starting to show its age. The Tin House was shipped to my grandfather during the Prohibition by a man who couldn't pay his bill. Oh, if the Tin House walls could talk! It's where they kept the moonshine during Prohibition. To this day, the willow tree and the Tin House are favored spots for weddings and parties. Pat and I were married at the Willow Tree in 1988. [See Chapter XI – Love & Marriage.] The willow tree is still the scene of weddings.

"Theodore, the handyman, taught me the ways of the hotel, and a lot about life. I admired him so much. He had his special set of tools for all the tasks he performed at the hotel. He did the work of five people. He put up the awning by himself, had tools for every step. He took good care of his tools. He had a ritual about sharpening his knives, and I'd watch him. Every Saturday, he'd grind all the knives down so he'd be ready to carve the roast beef on Sunday. He'd always be prepared for his tasks. He could put all the windows down for a storm or the season faster than a team of five.

"When my grandparents had the winter Chalfonte in Carolina, they shipped equipment back and forth in a boxcar. Theodore would load kitchen appliances, ovens, mixers, on a wagon and old stevedore horses pulled it to the train station where the Acme is now, and loaded it on the train. The next season, they did it all over again to travel back to Cape May.

"Theodore hosted wonderful beach picnics. He'd build a fire on the beach out at Higbee on the bay at the end of New England Road. He hauled everything out there – tables, linens, hotel china and cutlery. We'd have bowls of drawn butter, steamed shrimp, lobster, shucked raw clams, corn on the cob. When I returned to the hotel as an adult, and worked in maintenance, I acquired a four-wheel drive pickup that navigated the beach, making it easier to transport all the needs out there. We'd eat and watch the sunset, and the kids played games. The staff worked seven days a week, half a day on Sunday. There was no Sunday dinner at the hotel. The beach picnics were good for morale, the closeness of the staff. We were all family together.

"I have great memories of Dot's husband Burton. He was a fisherman. A massive man with the biggest hands. We had a big old pot –

16 gallons – in which they boiled the water for the sweet corn. He'd move that pot with boiling water with his bare hands from the back to the kitchen stove.

"You know that Helen, the cook, never measured anything. She had her secrets. Her secret for sweet corn – put some condensed milk in the water, but NEVER salt the water. Helen used Carnation canned milk in her spoon bread. When Cissy Finley was trying to get Helen to measure everything for the cookbook, Helen would sneak off sometimes, and she told me, 'I always leave out one secret ingredient.'

"The Hurricane Gloria flood was memorable. David Von Savage's wedding was scheduled for the weekend, and there was 16 inches of water in the lobby.

"I don't know how we did it, but we got the water out of the hotel – the lobby, dining room and kitchen. The dining room floor was still wet, and Jean Lloyd, a staffer, was on a ladder stringing garlands around the dining room. It was an epic day. Jean is the only person I know who could cry and laugh at a circumstance at the same time."

Judy Bartella "I loved Theodore. He could fix anything. He was an inventor. The inside of the toilets may have looked like a Rube Goldberg production, but they worked. Theodore didn't drive, and a cousin would drive him up for the season in this huge black Ford, cavernous, and filled with his tools. When the laundry truck came, Theodore grabbed the 30-pound bundles and ran them up the steps. Up and down and down and up. One day he invented a rope and pulley system to haul the bundles upstairs. Theodore's magic.

Phoebe Peyton Hanson "Henry (aka Bunches) was bellman and ran the lobby. Everyone loved Henry. He tended the candy counter in the lobby and answered questions. He knew everything about everything. All the streets, all the shops, the best beaches, the best fishing. One day someone asked for an encyclopedia. 'Why would you want an encyclopedia,' asked Henry. 'Ask me. I probably know the answer.'

Lucille Thompson *Daughter of Helen Dickerson; Chalfonte cook, formerly a waitress* "William, the maitre d', wore a tuxedo in the dining room and white gloves. He made a big ceremony of pulling out chairs for the mealtime guests. He made us – the wait staff – stand with our hands, in white gloves, behind our back until time to serve. He was very strict. In his old south way,

SHUTTERED
Cricket Satterfield waist high in salt water after the ocean breached the sea wall during Hurricane Gloria. He arrived to help clean up for a wedding the next day, held as scheduled.
Satterfield family collection

he had rules for everything; including how there should always be a serving plate beneath every serving of everything. He would say: 'Don't never serve nothin' on no naked plate.'

Anne LeDuc "Tommy Satterfield, Jim and Sarah Lee's son, was the resident prankster. He worked as a bellman for a number of years and charmed our guests. He had an infectious sense of humor and high jinx which made him popular with all of us."

HOTEL FIXTURE
An important part of Chalfonte life for many years, Henry Thatch ran the lobby and, as bellman, was responsible for ice and warm water in rooms.
Satterfield family collection

Remembering Mary "Diddy"
Christian Mulligan

Jim Abrams *Hotel Maintenance* "Diddy was from a fine old southern family in Huntingdon, West Virginia. Her parents were friends of the Satterfields. She's one of those who grew up at the Chalfonte. For her it was home, it was entertaining. She was a very attractive southern lady. When she was young, she was drop-dead gorgeous. Her parents were well off. Her husband had been in World War II. He became Secretary of the US Aeronautics Board and was a vice president of B&O Railroad and was instrumental in the restoration of the Washington, DC train station. Diddy had three children and lived in a beautiful home in Bethesda, Maryland. Yet she loved the Chalfonte, and being here. She was in charge of housekeeping, worked as hostess in the dining room. No matter the circumstances, Diddy never hurried. She floated across a room, and she immediately fascinated with her rather breathless southern speech pattern. Diddy could ask most anyone to do most anything, and the way she asked, just made you want to comply. She was lovely and she was generous. If someone was down on their luck, Diddy stepped in, and took care of it. She was very smart. People smart. And, she loved gossip. She was a big fan of tabloid news and was proud of it. She'd have the tabloids around and she loved the Jerry Springer show. She was intrigued with the human condition, especially celebrities. She got Bill Fralin, a college staffer who became a lawyer, hooked on tabloids and he used to subscribe to them and save them for Diddy and ship them to her at the hotel."

Still today, Bill Fralin supplies tabloid subscriptions at his Washington, DC law firm.

The following excerpt appeared in the article, "130 Years of Magic", by Susan Tischler in *Cape May Magazine* on July, 2006:

As Debra [Donahue, former public relations director] tells the story, "Diddy is a southern belle... She is a very elegant lady with a soft southern accent and she has a few endearing quirks. At age 65, she decided to get tattooed – butterfly tattoos – on her wrist, upper chest and shoulders. Why did she wait until 65?" 'Mother would have disapproved. She died.' And Diddy got tattooed.

At 86, Diddy was the Chalfonte's yard sale maven. Every Saturday morning, she would traverse the area looking for 'finds'. "And she would come back," says Debra, "with the most hor-

THE DEBUTANTE
Top: Diddy Christian Mulligan, a southern belle, spread her charm all around the Chalfonte compound. She's pictured in 1965 with Mary Sattler, left, and Diddy's mother Linda Christian, right.
Chalfonte collection

Above: Diddy, left, and friend Jean Mulvehill.
Chalfonte collection

rendous stuff you have ever seen." Mostly in the form of paintings. "If you call them that: Ballet dancers, clowns, Renoir knock-offs which Diddy maintained were obviously originals, velvet paintings and 'objects d'art'.

"Then she would come into my office," says Debra, "and ask me to make museum signs so she could hang these finds all over the hallway outside her room and in the women's [staff] bathroom down the hall. We call it Diddy's Gallery."

Still hanging outside her room is a "creepy

pink hat with plastic flowers on it." The sign reads: Hat worn by Princess Diana at a garden party at Buckingham Palace. Purchased by the Chalfonte at Christie's Auction for $10,000 (1997). Beneath the "scary" velvet painting the sign reads: Turkey Ottoman Empire 1500s. On loan from the Metropolitan Museum of Art (1990).

Thomas Bostwick "Wicky" McConnon
Acton, Massachusetts "My family was from Pittsburgh and we rented a cottage on Pittsburgh Avenue. Then we learned about the Chalfonte and the entire family stayed at the hotel for several years. I began working at the Chalfonte as a busboy when I was 15. I was one of the guest teenagers who filled in after the wage walkout in 1966. I begged my parents to allow me to complete the summer, which I did, for $15 a week plus room and board. (I think I came to understand what the work stoppage was about.)

"I begged Mrs Satterfield to allow me to return the next summer as a night watchman at $25 a week. I slept in the cupola and before my career ended, I was sleeping on a waterbed in the cupola. I sold waterbeds, as a matter of fact, from a 1951 Cadillac hearse. I had a friend who wanted the engine in the hearse for his Cadillac convertible. We bought the hearse for $600, and switched engines and the hearse became my vehicle with Grateful Dead stickers all over it. It was my and my friend Bayard

PARTY PROP
Sometimes Wicky McConnon's hearse was useful at cocktail hour: the McConnons and Straters in 1971.

BEACH PICNIC
A Sunday tradition was heading to Higbee's for a lobster bake: Anne LeDuc, Marge Stiegerwait, Tom McConnon.
Wicky McConnon collection

Stevens' transportation around Cape May. Mrs Satterfield said, 'Wicky, you keep that hearse out of sight and park it out back.' Guests had complained that seeing the hearse from dining room windows made them anxious or depressed. Its proximity to the Tin House made it a spot for guests to occasionally take their cocktails in the capacious and velvet-lined business end of the vehicle.

"The hearse became a legendary vehicle. Long-time guest Parks Duffy was invited to a party at his friend Jimmy Hechter's a couple blocks down Stockton Avenue. Mr Duffy borrowed an old door from Theodore. He got on the door and we slid him in the back of the hearse with two bottles of liquor crossed on his chest. Bellhops and waiters were enlisted as pallbearers. I wore my top hat. Mrs Satterfield and Mrs Nash, dressed in black, wearing veils, carrying handkerchiefs and bibles, rode in the hearse, sobbing and wailing, 'Oh, he was such a good man.' I inched the limousine toward the Hechters', followed by walking mourners and a parade of cars. Anne LeDuc remembers we had a police escort.

"Arriving at the Hechters', most of the guests were on the porch, and they had no clue why a funeral procession was stopping by. We pulled Mr Duffy from the back. He silently mounted the steps, eyes closed, and handed over the two bottles of liquor. Jimmy Hechter dissolved in laughter. I doubt Jimmy was ever able to best that prank in their long friendship of 'Can you top this?'

THE CHAUFFEUR
Wicky McConnon
and his 1971
hearse that was a
Chalfonte fixture
in the early 70s,
despite Meenie
Satterfield's
protests.
Wicky McConnon
collection

"My night watchman duties fit my schedule just fine. I made the rounds from midnight to 6am. Prime time was from midnight to 2am, when guests were returning from bars downtown. I herded them inside with as little noise as possible. I slept on my waterbed in the cupola late, until beach time, and then partied until midnight, when it was time to make my rounds again. Mrs Satterfield learned of the waterbed only at the end of a summer when I was draining it in the downspout and she wondered, 'Theodore, where is all this water coming from?'

"The Chalfonte was a bare bones institution where everyone made the best of everything, including at 5pm in the hallway, a line of people in bathrobes, with cocktails in their hands, waiting their turns in shared bathrooms."

Wicky McConnon's early entrepreneurial skills, selling waterbeds from a Cadillac hearse, paid off. He owns a software company and flies his own four-seat helicopter from the family horse farm in Massachusetts to their vacation home in New Hampshire, among other short hops. He started flying when he was 11. In recent years, he took up flying again. Just about the time he was going to buy a plane he decided instead to try out a chopper and that suited him better. He and his wife Rita-Marie pay annual visits to the Chalfonte with their sons Coleman,

SUMMERTIME
Above: Former Chalfonte co-owner Judy Bartella's family reunited and worked at the Chalfonte. Judy is in the foreground with brother Sims, left, Brenda Bartella, center, and her son Mark Bartella.

BEACH LUNCH
Center: Judy Bartella hosts a get-together including Nancy Dowlin in hat, sister Cathy Kriss and step-mother Brenda Bartella in dark glasses.
Judy Bartella Collection

THE GIRLS' CLUB
Opposite: Brenda Bartella Peterson hosts her friends for a girls' getaway at the hotel. Left to right: Tracy Parker, Rosemary Wimpling, Lisa Johnston, Rhonda Johnston, Brenda, Martha Johnston Dryden, Mary Henson.
Brenda Bartella Peterson

Andrew, Tom and his wife Kristie and in 2010, baby Lilah.

Cathy McConnon *Philadelphia, Pennsylvania; Wicky's sister* "As kids we grew up at the Chalfonte in summer and we couldn't wait to be old enough to work at the hotel, as all our older friends did. I was in charge of the Children's Dining Room. I worked the front desk with Alice Satterfield [Tor], Meenie's granddaughter.

"I remember our salary was $19 a week, but that included room and board, and I had a very good room. I developed a routine of working as a Kelly Girl in Florida in the winter and at the Chalfonte in summer. I came in from the beach one day and Meenie was having trouble with the payroll. I said, 'Let me take a look at it.' All the salaries were paid in cash after taxes were taken out. So I took all the cash to my room, and it was hot. I couldn't turn on the fan because money would fly all over the place. I sorted the cash and filled the envelopes for workers and that became one of my jobs. I recall that the Chalfonte in those days cashed a lot of checks for guests. It didn't matter the amount. It was a service because everyone knew everyone else. Meenie made her presence in the lobby and if she didn't like the looks of someone she would give a nod and that meant no.

"Did my brother Wicky tell you that our

mother Bossy [nickname for Bostick] drove his hearse all the way from Pittsburgh to Cape May? When I worked for an insurance company in Boston I missed the Chalfonte crowd so much I'd catch a flight to Philadelphia. I parked my car at a gas station at the Platt Bridge, and made arrangements for a pickup at Philadelphia airport, and then drive on down to Cape May. That's real love for the place."

Brenda Bartella Peterson *Raleigh, North Carolina; Judy Bartella's stepmother* "The Chalfonte is so much more than a hotel. I hope the Chalfonte is treated as the leading lady. She has a personality, an aura of her own. She is so precious to me and my boys, such an important part of our lives. All three of us – Mark, Sims and myself – worked at the hotel. Bart [Judy's father] and I first visited the hotel in the 70s. Bart was a very large man, 6-5, and we stayed in the Bridal Suite, one of the only rooms with a bathtub. We have a picture of big Bart in that tiny tub. We dressed for cocktails on the balcony of the suite, and Bart appears in polyester bright yellow trousers and a bright yellow sports shirt. We are joined by Meenie and Martha, who stretches but 4-10. Martha, in her 80s, craned her neck back and examined the full length of him and declared, 'Well, sir, if you like yellow, you got a bargain.'

"Judy's father thought she was making a big

> **"The Chalfonte was a bare bones institution where everyone made the best of everything, including at 5pm in the hallway, a line of people in bathrobes, with cocktails in their hands, waiting their turns in shared bathrooms."**

mistake buying the hotel. But the Chalfonte would become a member of our family.

"My teenage son Mark, after his father's death, was having a very tough time, lethargic and depressed. He just could not get his act together. His girlfriend went abroad for a year of study and she told him if when she came back he was still languishing, their relationship was over. He packed up his car and headed to the Chalfonte, where he spent a year. He got off pot and got his life together, locking horns with Anne LeDuc more than once. I think working for the hotel that year really set him straight.

"One summer I worked as a hostess in the dining room. It was total fun. I heard all the Chalfonte stories that get passed along – one generation to another. The stories become legend and who knows what the truth is, but it doesn't matter what the truth is. The larger truth is that the Chalfonte has given us all those rich moments – of hilarity, humor.

"I was always the glamour girl, who married Bart, 32 years older than me, and in my 50s I became an ordained minister of the Christian Church [the Disciples of Christ]. A group of women from a church in Kentucky join me every year for a Chalfonte visit. We all love to dress, dance and laugh. We have a reputation for being wild party girls, but that happens to be one of those exaggerated Chalfonte legends.

"I have lived through everything life can dish out. I have gone there to be alone, to just sit on the porch, to walk on the beach. I have gone to the Chalfonte for healing. It was 2001 and my son Mark, 25, had graduated from college and was about to start, with full tuition, the best law school. He was involved in an all-terrain vehicle accident. It took his life. The staff who knew him that summer he got his act together at the hotel arranged for a brass plate remembering Mark. It's on one of the rockers."

Caroline "Copie" Copland *Pittsburgh* "I was 18, wanting a job at the beach. I was talking to a girlfriend who the previous summer had been a babysitter for Nancy Satterfield Davey's son Bart. I said I am going to apply for that job. I wrote a letter to Mrs Satterfield, and she said that job was taken. She said the head of the Children's Dining Room job was open. I took it. I hopped a direct flight from Pittsburgh to Cape May, not knowing one soul. I met Meenie and she said, 'I think I am going to like you, but you talk too fast.' I never have conquered that trait, talking too fast. I managed the Children's Dining Room for two years, and later on worked in reservations. This has become my second home. I have helped close up for the season, worked as a chambermaid. The schedule couldn't be better for the beach person that I am."

Linda McCrary *Tahlequah, Oklahoma* "I have often been accused of flying by the seat of my pants but I assure you, the Chalfonte adventure is at the top of the list. It's 1982. I had left social work in Oklahoma after 15 years, spent five months in Boston with friends and when the weather turned cold, headed south for the winter in my little red Honda. Stopping along the way at islands and lighthouses, I met some people who suggested not missing Cape May and taking the ferry to Delaware and heading on south.

"Got a room at the Mad Batter, and traveled around town on my bicycle and fell instantly in love with Cape May. I wondered into the Chalfonte, met George at the front desk who had lots of time to talk because the hotel had closed for the season. He told me about Anne and Judy's efforts to preserve and keep the hotel operating. That winter I wrote letters to innkeepers applying for work, and Anne was the first to respond. We agreed to meet on the front porch the first work weekend in May. We got along famously and I moved into the hotel that night and have

THE MAN
Jim Abrams has a passion for antiques and old buildings. He works as a staff member restoring the Chalfonte and coordinates projects for work weekends.
Chalfonte collection

been moving in and out to this day more times than I can remember. That was 27 years ago.

"That first year I was hostess in the dining room and worked from April to October. As we served family style, it was my job to convince guests to share tables with other guests. My social work skills came in quite handy. I worked a few weeks or a month at a time each season until 1993 when I came back for three full years,

CHALFONTE BUDDIES
Chalfonte artist Lou Riccio and long-time staffer Cathy McConnon. Cathy knew every guest for years.
Lou Riccio

even staying one winter in the Howard Street Cottage next door.

"The wait staff was hard-drinking and some times I had to roll them out of bed and into the dining room in time to serve breakfast. Many of the ex-staff frequent the hotel as guests and also have reunions there. It is really fun to see how they have grown and prospered (well some of them).

"Back then we still had guests who would stay a month or more at the hotel. Elwis Starr and her brother Dick Sattler, from St. Louis, who had been guests as children, began to come back frequently and became my first fast friends. Elwis has since passed away, but Dick continues to come every August and has a group he meets there: Ron and Jule Campbell, Cindy and George Waters and Crissy Walford. Lifelong relationships have been forged there. I am true testament to that.

"Meenie Satterfield was in residence the first summer I worked at the hotel. She and Martha Nash, her lifelong friend and longtime housekeeper at the hotel, resided in what was known as "the family hall" [where offices are now located]. I became buddies with Martha and Meenie. Both octogenarians walked with canes, but made the twice daily trek to the dining room.

"If Meenie wanted to talk to you she would hit the wooden floor with her cane and motion for you. She did that frequently that summer as both ladies were always very curious about the new guests. I would head for the Family Hall after breakfast to fill them in on all the previous night's gossip (of which there was ample to share and of course for some stories, I used my discretion).

"Both ladies loved to comment on the 'unacceptable attire' in the dining room, which had a dress code back then. Men were asked to wear shirts with collars at breakfast and jackets for dinner. It was quite difficult for the ladies to accept any change on that policy. We served Sunday dinner at noon and gentlemen were still required to wear jackets, but were allowed to place them on the back of their chairs after being seated. It was not easy to live with this policy on really hot August days when people had to come back from the beach and don that jacket (usually seersucker). The policy was so important that we even had loaners for those who forgot or had not been 'properly informed'. Eldred Morris, the hotel's front desk manager, initiated this policy.

Meenie and Martha loved seeing the gentlemen in jackets. One of the ladies' favorite guests during that time was Bill Lillard. Bill was also from Richmond and was a real southern gentleman, attested to by his seersucker suits, Richmond drawl and penchant for Jim Beam. Oh, those Richmond people love their bourbon. Cocktail hour at the Tin House was started by Meenie years ago and is still a part of the Chalfonte routine. An invite to the Tin House has sealed many a longtime friendship and sometimes may have ended a few if you ask me."

* * *

Kathy Kennison Barker, who now lives in St Paul, Missouri, was an Iowa girl, born on a farm near Mason City, the same town that produced writer Meredith Willson, of Music Man fame. On a dare, she got a job delivering Winnebago campers (manufactured in Iowa) all over the US. She learned of Cape May and the Chalfonte in the most circuitous way and begged for a dispatch to New Jersey. Instead she got a trip to Connecticut, caught a bus to Cape May, arriving just in time for Hurricane Gloria.

Excerpts from Kathy's' essay, "Finding the Pink Hotel"...

"I arrived in the middle of the night on the New Jersey Transit with my worldly possessions in a duffle bag. Unable to find a cab, I dragged the overloaded bag to the hotel from the Acme parking lot. A lithe creature with a throaty voice, and wearing an elegantly simple little black dress and sandals, slinked toward me from the front desk and gave me the first of many lists from Anne. Anne's list included a good night's rest, settling into my room, and dinner prep duty the following afternoon.

"My watch quit running that first day. How appropriate. Consequently I was late in getting to the back alley for dinner prep. I felt terrible about being late for my first task, which was to shuck corn, compounded by the fact I had no idea how to shuck corn. I told Anne LeDuc I had never prepared corn for cooking and she was dumbfounded. 'Aren't you from Iowa?' she asked. I confirmed that I was indeed an Iowan. She asked, 'How do you prepare corn for cooking in Iowa?' I told her, 'I open a can.'

"My first day off, three weeks later, I awak-

From The Archives

Excerpt from The Chalfonte Newsletter, Summer 1978:
In Memory of Theodore Roosevelt Jackson: April 8, 1900 – March 15, 1978

Theodore was a member of the Chalfonte staff and family for over 40 years. We shall all miss him greatly, for as a guest wrote us: "Theodore was a real fixture, his head popping in the lobby to receive his next assignment or silently materializing in the Playroom with the world's largest flashlight (to unlock the door of his room). He was a real gentleman in his shy way. He seemed to fumble for words and yet you knew what he meant. He knew a lot about fish, and the weather, and all kinds of practical matters and if you pressed him, he would open up a bit. I envied him his delight in gadgets and tools – and his car that he rarely drove is a real classic, and so was Theodore!

ened to the sounds of hammers pounding and the thuds of boards and plywood sheets being stacked in the back alley. The awnings were being rolled up and the rickety shutters, with the peeling green paint, were being closed. I discovered shutters were not for aesthetics, but to protect the windows during storms. Hurricane Gloria was making her way to New Jersey.

"I'll never forget the sound, or lack of sound, of the last generator going silent as Cricket flipped the switch at the breaker. All the scurrying of the day was done, and it was time to go, to get out of town. We had one last task. Did anyone put up Martha's pillow? Mrs Nash always sat on a little round pillow we placed on her chair at the family table. I ran back into the dining room, retrieved the pillow and placed it on the buffet. We were ready to go.

"Most of us piled into two cars and headed toward Anne's house in Moorestown. All I remember is darkness and blinding rain, and wondering what on earth I'd do if I got separated from Anne. We were directed to our designated sleeping areas. My accommodations were the living room, which I was to share with the mother of the Chinese opera singer whom Anne

and Judy hired as a roofer. I think the woman's name was Ting Ting. Ting Ting made a beeline for the couch and I got the window seat.

"I awakened to the sounds of voices in the kitchen and the fragrance of bacon and eggs. Cricket and the kitchen manager had come in a third vehicle with provisions. Our eyes were fixed on the TV as the furious storm made its way up the Jersey coast. We could hear the wind getting fierce and the rain was pelting. Just then we heard a loud crack and shattering glass. I think we all knew what happened. Our worst fears confirmed – a giant tree limb lay across Eldred's beloved car.

"Previously Anne and Judy [co-owner] had made a date for a meeting with the father of the bride for a wedding reception that was to be held the following day. We had to be there for that

BIRTHDAY GIRL
Jane Reid of Charlotte, North Carolina at her Chalfonte birthday party. Her two sons worked at the hotel.

FRIENDS
Top right: Margaret Grove and Mary Jo Douglas, a guest who enjoyed hotel summers so much she became a staff member in charge of laundry.

CHALFONTE COUSINS
Opposite: Calvin Satterfield IV and cousin Tommy Satterfield, right, spent childhood summers at the hotel.
Lou Riccio

meeting! Never mind the three-to-four-feet of water around the hotel through which we had to wade. Never mind the three-to-four-feet of sea just subsided in the dining room. Never mind the cans of grease washed over the kitchen, leaving the floors slicker than ice. Judy offered to go by boat and pick up sandwiches before we started cleaning. Has anyone noticed there's no electricity and darkness is coming?

"These crazy Easterners! In less than 24 hours we were open for business. We pulled the last of the seaweed from the bushes. The dining room is festooned with flowers. The wedding is on. The battle-weary troops, fresh from showers after two days of intense cleanup, stand by the double doors of the kitchen waiting to enter the dining room with our trays of culinary delights.

"Other Chalfonte benefits: Three sets of ears in the kitchen to help sooth ruffled feathers with southern fried chicken and spoonbread. Who needs a therapist when you've got the ladies of the Chalfonte kitchen? Sometimes we ran the entire hotel from the kitchen.

"Anne fired me the summer I quit. She looked me straight in the eye and said, 'I will not have quitters on this team.' Then she took me to lunch and suggested I go home to Iowa to be with my terminally ill father.

"I worked on and off at the Chalfonte for nine years. What was the draw? Those grand ladies located in a time and a place where watches don't need to run and life is stranger than fiction. It's humbling to recognize the number of lives that are touched by Anne's relentless efforts to preserve the traditions of the Chalfonte.

"The accommodations I was told very early on are secondary to ambiance. It's about people: Anne and the Chalfonte and all those quirky and wonderful characters of the hotel."
Wynne Milner *Chadds Ford, Pennsylvania*
"John and I came to Cape May in summertime

ever since we were first married. We rented a little apartment around the corner from the Chalfonte, so we knew of it.

"John, an architect, became a consultant for the building, and one of the first volunteer efforts his University of Pennsylvania students did was paint the porch on a weekend.

"We stayed in touch and Anne LeDuc and Judy Bartella asked me if I, a teacher and off in the summer, would come down and help. I worked as a reservations person, a night auditor, front desk clerk, dining room hostess, and as a kitchen manager. I didn't live at the hotel. John and I rented an apartment on the east end and I biked back and forth. John came down on weekends. He organized the first wine list and bought and served the wines. I enjoyed my time in the kitchen the best. I gathered all the fresh produce, all the fruits and vegetables from local markets, especially Alice's on Broadway. I went to the fish market. I came up with ideas to feed the youngsters in the Children's Dining Room, and prepared dinners for the staff. The Chalfonte tradition was a turkey dinner once a week. I took the leftover turkey and made a Julia Child's turkey casserole, or Tetrazinni. It was a favorite of the staff and I have used the recipe over the years for my guests.

"There are many Chalfonte stories. As a reservations clerk, taking phone calls, I was on the phone with a gentleman reserving for a family group. There were multiple parts. There were children so they would be in the Annex. There were family members who could not navigate stairs. The gentleman became very impatient. I said, 'Sir I am sorry I am taking so long, but I want to make sure you are comfortable.' He said, 'Miss, I have been coming to the Chalfonte all of my life, and I have never been comfortable.'

"On the front desk one day, a man checked in and the bellhop took his bag up and the man comes down, and said, 'There is something wrong with my bed.' I asked the bellhop to go upstairs and find out what was the matter. The bellhop found a shutter under the mattress!"

Linda Lloyd Larson *Boise, Utah* "I took the summer off after closing a bakery I started with a friend in Cape May and was sitting on the deck talking to a neighbor, Wynne Milner, who was volunteering at the hotel in 1985. Wynne said they were in need of help and I had always been fascinated by the hotel, and started as a waitress. I went on to work in public relations, marketing, booking weddings and special events.

CHALFONTE DEVOTEES
Wynne and John Milner volunteered their expertise at the hotel in the 80s. John, a University of Pennsylvania professor of architecture, introduced student work weekends and later developed a hotel wine list. Wynne, a gourmet cook, worked in the kitchen and dining room.
Milner family collection

"The architecture is the bones of the experience. The building is gorgeous, gracious, welcoming, unpredictable and cranky at times. I grew up spending a month every summer with my grandmother in an old rambling house on North Street. I realized when my family sold our summer place how a well-loved building keeps your past alive. The Chalfonte does that. It holds some of my best memories. John and I had our wedding reception at the Chalfonte October 20th, 1990 – already 20 years ago!"

* * *

There's a daily freshness about Nancy Granick, the Chalfonte's General Manager, that makes it implausible to imagine she has worked at the Chalfonte for 18 years, since 1993, and has been general manager for 15 years. Her chance encounter with the hotel has been directed by fate, as have been the relationships of many other staffers and the Chalfonte.

Nancy Granick "I was working in Philadelphia at a corporate restaurant with Dan Walker, who had some experience in the Chalfonte kitchen when he was in college. Quite coin-

cidentally, I earlier had read the *Philadelphia Inquirer* and noted Miss Helen's obituary and thought, what a story this is! I mentioned it to Dan, and he said, 'Oh, you would love this place – the Chalfonte – and Cape May.' I had never been to the Jersey shore.

"That summer of 93 Dan got itchy to move on. He called Anne LeDuc and was hired. I took his job in Philadelphia. We'd talk and he'd say he had been on break: had just taken a nap, been out horseback riding, had a great swim at the beach. I thought, what is this? Here I am in the city, working 24 hours a day.

"Dan invited me down. I took the bus. I was walking to the hotel and got to the corner of Columbia and Howard, and looked up and there she is! I said, 'Oh, I am not ever leaving!' I stayed for four days and met everyone and sat at the family table with Anne and Nancy Wyatt and was impressed with Anne. She was very spicy.

"I was enchanted, but needed to return to Philadelphia and work. It's July and suddenly my restaurant closed. Dan called and said why don't you get out of the city and come down for

SNAPSHOT
Public relations and marketing director Debra Donahue, Jane Perna, Nancy Wyatt, general manager Nancy Granick, Anne LeDuc, Tammy Carbone, wedding coordinator Terry Carr.
Photograph by Judy Bartella

HOTEL FAMILY
Opposite, top: Alice Satterfield Tor and husband Duner. Alice is a daughter of Maria and Calvin III and now summers nearby.
Mary Minor Taylor

Opposite, below: Jessica Rubenstein Katz, Susan Sullivan Neubauer and Travis Clay. Susan vacationed at the Chalfonte every year and later became a staff member. She was matron of honor at her sister Amanda's wedding.

a couple weeks. And, ever since, I've never really left. I became the dining room manager, worked other jobs, then became general manager.

"Anne LeDuc afforded me an education in management and customer service. We went to classes and seminars. The very best part of this job is the people. I enjoy putting together the staff each season, but the highlight is the return of the guests who've been gathering here for decades, generations. We are all one big family.

"This summer [2010] Ali Naqvi, who had his and his wife Linda's whole family here, sat down next to me and said, 'How do you get all these nice people to work here?' I said, 'Ali, I don't do a darn thing, the building does it. This ol' girl collects these people.' She does have a way about her. This time of year, as the season ends, she gets tired as we all do, and she wilts and says, 'It's time for all of you to get out of here. I need my rest.'

"But then miraculously, in spring, she shakes herself off and pulls herself up as the work weekends come around, and becomes the leading lady again."

CHAPTER X

Art & Artists
At The Chalfonte

*T*IS early September and the day is overcast. Autumn Clematis vines, their tiny white flowers blooming in white clouds, hang heavy on the rose fence by the Tin House. Their fragrance is intoxicating. Labor Day has come and gone and a peace has settled over the Chalfonte compound.

Positioned around the property are a dozen or so artists. Some have chosen to work in the alley. They are intent on their compositions, eyeing the old Chowder Hall, the Peasants' Palace and Franklin Street Cottage for the structure of their watercolors. Marge Chavooshian, the teacher, sits on a small stool, pencil in hand, explaining to a student the measurement of an eave spout to a shutter. She uses a squinting technique, pencil in hand on an outstretched arm, to determine height-to-width dimensions. She dots with a pencil the starting points of windows, doors, shutters and other details, and pencils in shadow lines before considering her watercolor palette.

Marge, from Trenton, New Jersey has been conducting plein air workshops at the Chalfonte for 25 years. Her relationship with the hotel began one vacation day when she was sitting between two cars in order to capture a particular angle. Anne LeDuc and Judy Bartella were new Chalfonte owners. They liked what they saw on Marge's easel and asked if she would consider exhibiting her work in the lobby. The exhibits led to workshops and annual one-woman shows in the dining room. Marge has painted more than 100 versions of the Chalfonte and each season the old hotel inspires new views.

Marge Chavooshian "I have always been drawn to the drama of the Chalfonte's shapes and shadows. The more complicated the structure – of which the Chalfonte is one – the more challenging to express different values and different shapes. No matter where you turn at the Chalfonte – the complex façade, the columns, the long porch, the cupola, the windows, the doors, The Tin House, the Secret Garden, the Solarium – each and all provide charming views.

"When the sunlight hits the building, it is glowing. It's all crisp and clean and the nuances of patterns that happen in the shadow and light are appealing to the artist."

Marge learned to draw during early training

at the Art Students League in New York City. She has traveled extensively in Europe, painting in parks, on streets and waterfronts. She is the recipient of more than 155 regional and national awards. Her paintings are in private and corporate collections here and abroad.

* * *

Marie Natale, of Egg Harbor Township, New Jersey, has been painting the Chalfonte since 2001. She had her first show in the Magnolia Room in 2004 and has been featured in the hotel's advertising since it was purchased by the Mullock family in 2008.

Marie Natale "What draws me to the Chalfonte is observing the light changes as each hour passes during the day. The white building glows anew in shadows and reflects light of pink tones from the red tin roof and cool green shadows from the striped awnings on the porch.

CHALFONTE LIFE
Watercolor artist Marge Chavooshian is the most prolific of the artists who love to paint the old hotel. Marge has been painting Chalfonte scenes and teaching workshops at the hotel for 25 years. Opposite: " The Secret Garden" and "Good Morning." Previous page: "So this is the Chalfonte."

The chapter opening page features a detail from Marie Natale's "Break Time".

The sun on the white produces golden tones. I strive to push color in my work, inviting viewers to see the Chalfonte through my artist's eyes. The Chalfonte's sense of southern charm and extended family keeps me connected. Emotionally, the Chalfonte is home to me. I am drawn to the kitchen and Dot and Lucille and painting them as they work at their special cooking talents."

Marie is known for her vibrant color palette. She has been painting since age 12, has a master's degree in art education from Rowan University and taught in public schools for 10 years. She is a signature artist of the Noyes Museum in Oceanville and Hammonton, New Jersey, teaches watercolor at workshops in Cape May, at the Ocean City Art Center, Gloucester County Community College, and art guilds along the East Coast.

FROM THE ROOFTOP
Marie Natale never tires of the Chalfonte vistas.
Each day is a new experience in reflected sea
light and shadows. Above: "Break Time" (a view
of the rooftops and back alley, as seen from the
cupola).
Opposite: "Fine Dining on the Chalfonte Porch".

marie natale NWS

Alice Steer Wilson (1926-2001) and the Chalfonte enjoyed a long and special relationship. Alice, with her affection for architectural treasures, had been painting the Chalfonte for years. Her painting, "From One Generation to Another", says in watercolor what words cannot convey about the dozens of families who consider the hotel their summer home for as many as four and five generations.

Longtime Chalfonte owner Anne LeDuc was

MASTER CLASS
Alice Steer Wilson's watercolor "From One Generation to Another".
From the collection of Joan T. Chance. Copyright 1998, Alice Steer Wilson Family Trust. All rights reserved.

BELOVED ARTIST
Alice Steer Wilson had many successful art shows at the Chalfonte. Alice is pictured, left, with friend Libby Bellangy.
Photograph by Janice Wilson Stridick

an aficionado of Alice's art. On walks around town, Anne saw Alice painting, especially in the light at the end of the day. After Alice's death in 2001, Laura Albert wrote a memorial tribute in which Anne is quoted: "I can't put words to her artwork. Alice as a person meant the most to me, because she was just so vibrant and warm, and just had such a twinkle in her eye... and a great sense of humor, very human... very interested in all kinds of causes; one of the warmest, kindest people I have ever known."

Ten years earlier, Anne and co-owner Judy Bartella had suggested that Alice exhibit a one-woman show in the Magnolia Room. "For Mother the Chalfonte was a natural, wonderful venue," says daughter, Janice Wilson Stridick. "It was a lovely gathering place for Mother's audience that knew her, for her friends and new admirers. Sales of her work helped preserve the building, a National Historic Landmark, and her son-in-law Paul Stridick, an architect, helped hang the show. My background in marketing allowed for giving the shows themes and a series of postcards of her work announcing her shows. It was a family event."

The Magnolia Room exhibition became a Labor Day weekend ritual. The first was a rather modest affair. The second year, with Janice's urging, was a big event, with the Chalfonte staff putting out a beautiful spread of finger foods and beverages. "Mother felt she had to fill the room," says Janice, "and it motivated her to produce five or 10 full-sheet paintings, 15 or 20 middle-size ones and a bunch of little ones."

A TOUCH OF WHIMSY
Penny Chiusano catches the funky side of the hotel in her watercolor and collage combinations.

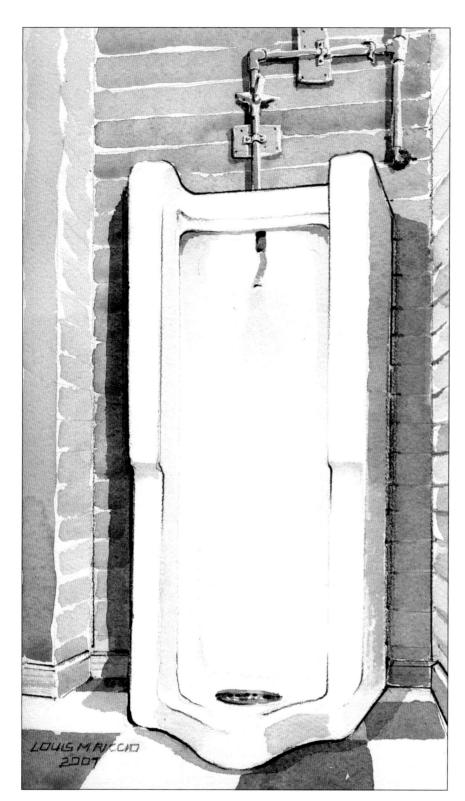

Laura Albert remembered in her memorial tribute: "The public's familiarity and accessibility to Wilson's work grew in 1977, when she and her husband Fred began printing note cards of her watercolor images of the town. Some of these included her favorite scenes, such as the dunes, the Grey Ghost and St Mary by-the-Sea at Cape May Point."

INSIDE AND OUT
Paintings by Lou Riccio include, clockwise from above: "The Big Boy" (a portrait of the men's room urinal), " Chalfonte Rocker", "Chalfonte Alley", "Secret Garden", "The Tin House".

In 1979, Alice and Fred bought one of the original Cape May buildings, the 1848 Steiner Cottage on Congress Street. Sometimes, Janice recalls, after she and her brother and sisters were grown, their mother would stay on at the beach house until December, because she loved to paint Cape May in the fall. Cape May, with its magnificent sea-lit colors and charm, became Alice's favorite artistic subject.

At the last Magnolia Room show Alice attended, all but three of her paintings were sold in the first half hour.

Alice Steer Wilson studied at the Pennsylvania Academy of Fine Arts. Throughout her career, she received an extensive list of awards and citations. Her work has been purchased by collectors throughout the United States and in Europe, and more than one million of her note cards have been sold.

* * *

Penny Chiusano, an artist from Pelham Manor, New York is a watercolorist whose whimsical paintings include pen-and-ink messages and collage.

Penny Chiusano "Ah, the Chalfonte. It is my place. My hotel. She is the grande dame of Cape May. She is the only hotel in town with integrity as far as I am concerned.

"I have been showing my art at the hotel for 15 years. But it was 25 years ago that my nose led me to this favorite place of mine. We were going

to the beach in 1985. We're in the car, a cooler packed with beer and wine and snacks, and we got caught in a traffic jam and it took three and a half hours to get over the George Washington Bridge.

"Our reservations are half a block from the Chalfonte, at the Dormer House, and I discover from my allergies that at that time they allowed pets. I am so allergic and so miserable among the cat and dog hair, I slept in the bathtub and as I awake in the morning, I smell Helen and Dot's breakfast. Like a bloodhound I track the smell to the Chalfonte and we have breakfast there and it is divine. The place is a wreck, all peeling and puckering then, before Anne and Judy's restorations. I stay there and fall in love with Chalfonte style and watch the place come back to life over the years.

"Six years ago I had cancer and as I lay in radiation, I transported my mind to the Solarium, the Chalfonte's lovely room of white and light, and imagine I am there. Then I got a call from Anne LeDuc. Now, she is the boss lady of the Chalfonte and a sometime curmudgeon. And she asked how was I? I was so touched. And I told her my mind trick of being in the Solarium, and she said, 'Just know that we are there with you.' I felt so embraced.

"I did go with Anne and my Chalfonte friends to the Solarium in my mind, every time I was in radiation. Anne called me every week to see how I was doing. I have gone through life and death in that hotel. It is part of my heart and soul. I brought my child, my son Timm, to that hotel when he was in third grade with one of his friends. And the next season there were many more friends to the point of eight friends. We would take the train to Atlantic City and get a limo to Cape May. The limo would pull up with all these boys tumbling out. Jackets were required at dinner and the boys scrounged in a closet by the bar for borrowed jackets that smelled of 1930s cigars.

"Now these are city kids who eat a lot of pizza and they are in the dining room with their hair slicked back and sitting up straight, drowning in their musty jackets, minding their manners, being served a full-course southern dinner, eating every bite and loving every moment. Now those boys are men and return with their wives, including my Timm and his wife Kelly.

"My husband Tom seldom visits the Chalfonte. He is too type A. He can't handle the quiet. It was he who for more than 20 years was How-

CHANCE ENCOUNTER
Linda McCrary was passing through town, happened into the Grande Dame of Howard Street and stayed on for staff work and a great place to paint. Above: "The Old Coal Bin" and, opposite, "View From Lenny's House".

RUG HOOKERS
Opposite: Ellen Savage's wonderfully detailed rug depicting the Chalfonte – she is a member of a group of rug hookers who annually visited the hotel.

ard Stern's general manager at K-Rock Radio."

Penny's watercolors are represented by the Amsterdam Whitney Gallery in Chelsea, New York City.

* * *

Lou Riccio *Malvern, Pennsylvania and West Cape May, New Jersey* "The Chalfonte has a wonderful character. Every angle, every light changes. It's almost like looking at the ocean. Every day there is a different light, a different shadow, a different tone. You never see the same set twice. It is a lovely piece of architecture with all of those nooks and crannies.

"My wife Linda worked at the Chalfonte since she was college age, and it was she who started me painting there. She requested several paintings of Helen, the cook, and subsequently I painted the rocking chairs, the Secret Garden,

the Tin House, the cupola.

"I had my first show in the Magnolia Room in 2010 and am painting toward another. Anne LeDuc, always a patron of the arts, surprised me with a check for some lessons with a watercolorist with whom I had been studying."

It isn't only painters who are drawn to the old hotel. Ellen Savage, an artist from Pottstown, Pennsylvania worked on a rug pattern designed by Beverly Conway.

Ellen Savage "This rug is 36 by 53 inches and it took me six months to finish hooking it. I stayed at it most every day except for two weeks when I got a stiff neck from working on it. The Chalfonte is a wonderful place for us to gather as artists, exchange ideas and materials and actually do the hooking in the dining room. We take over the place and we're welcomed to do that."

Art And Artists At The Chalfonte   221

Jilline Ringle, the "red-hot mama", amused audiences with her cabaret comedy acts and wowed them with her voice. Chalfonte collection

Michael Grasso, internationally recognized magician, played the Henry Sawyer Room in summer 2010. Photograph by Linda Arredondo, lindaarredondo.com

Cultural Centerpiece

THE Chalfonte became an oasis for the arts during the LeDuc-Bartella reign. Anne explains their cultural mission: "From the beginning of our ownership, Judy and I wanted to share the hotel with the cultural activities – and a wide range of them. Over time, we developed a cultural centerpiece."

Theater productions at the Chalfonte started with Michael Laird, a professional actor and director, who went on to be founder of the now well-established Cape May Stage. Laird produced cabaret shows at the hotel featuring, among others, Jilline Ringle, famous for her one-woman shows and singing ability. At six-two, she was literally a towering talent, and enjoyed being called "a red-hot mama."

For many summers, Chalfonte guests enjoyed performances of the Savoy Company, the oldest amateur theater group in Philadelphia. The troupe is dedicated to performing Gilbert and Sullivan operettas in "the original manner." There was nothing quite so delightful as hearing the sounds of opera pouring from the old gingerbread hotel.

Judy and Anne initiated a classical music series, Concerts by Candlelight, featuring fine musicians from the Philadelphia scene. Anne says one of her favorite memories is of very young children being taught how to play a violin on stage at a candlelight concert.

There were magic shows on the lawn for youngsters. More recently, Michael Grasso

The talented Festive Brass ensemble was one of many fine frequent musical features at the Chalfonte. Left to right: Nancy Dowlin, Joan Dowlin, Debra Taylor, Pete Krill, Barbara Prugh. Several of the Festive Brass musicians still perform in summer concerts and have been playing at the Chalfonte for 25 seasons. Judy Bartella collection

performed in the Henry Sawyer Room. He combines classic stage manipulation with live music and became a finalist in the popular TV show, *America's Got Talent*. He performs in nightclubs all around the US and had a successful tour of India.

The Chalfonte has hosted Victorian dance fests and dinners, piano concerts, journal writing, murder mystery weekends, folk and bluegrass, play readings, poetry workshops, puppet performances, "Gone with the Wind" and "Academy Award" hotel parties, artful craft camps for quilting and rug hooking.

The rug hookers' formal name is Rugs by the Sea, but they call themselves The Hookers. The group, mostly from the Mid-Atlantic states, has been holding week-long camps at the Chalfonte for more than 20 years – no other hotel would have them. Their rug shows are in the lobby, reading and Queen Anne rooms. The intricacy of the rugs is amazing – especially a rug that depicts the old lady herself, in all her quirky magnificence.

The Savoy Opera Company performed Gilbert and Sullivan operettas at the hotel.

CHAPTER XI
A History Of Romance

THE Chalfonte has a romantic mystery about it and a long history of love stories. Perhaps it's the lacy verandas, the Romeo and Juliet balconies or its appearance as a giant intricately decorated wedding cake, but brides and grooms are enamored with the place for their nuptials.

The Chalfonte has been a setting for weddings for almost a century, perhaps longer. Calvin and Susie Satterfield's daughter Phoebe chose the hotel for her wedding reception September 25, 1917.

The bridegroom, Thomas Peyton, was a First Lieutenant in the US Army. Peyton traveled to Cape May from Arizona, where he was on border patrol due to issues with Mexican General Poncho Villa. A year earlier, General Villa had ordered 500 revolutionary troops to cross the

CRICKET WEDS
Above: Patricia Murray and Cricket Satterfield married on September 18,1988. On the right is Lee Satterfield Probst, Cricket's daughter, who worked at the Chalfonte for years. Right: Cricket and his father James Morris Satterfield on the steps of Franklin Cottage. Opposite: Bon vivant Cricket surrenders to his bride, roped for good.
Satterfield family collection

WEDDING DESTINATION
Previous page: The Chalfonte is a favorite wedding site in Cape May, one of the country's most popular wedding destinations. Bride Angela Post is from Peru – her family traveled to the hotel for her wedding on August 15, 2009.
Photograph by Ray Hennessy

border into New Mexico. The Villistas attacked a US cavalry regiment, seizing horses and mules. They set the town of Columbus on fire. When the gunfire ended, there were many casualties on both sides. Lietuenant Peyton traveled from his border patrol to Cape May, with a stop on the way."

Phoebe Peyton Hanson Father was a classmate of Dwight Eisenhower at West Point. En route to his wedding he stopped in New Orleans for a night on the town with Ike. It must have been quite a party because father did reference it years later. They were very good friends. When I was an adult, after Ike became a general and my husband Bill was a base commander, we had

WEDDING TRADITION
Susie Satterfield's daughter Phoebe and Thomas Peyton had their wedding reception at the Chalfonte in 1917. Sister Lindsay "Tyee" was maid of honor.
Phoebe Peyton Hanson

dinner with Ike in Puerto Rico. It was a festive occasion with dancing, and a very good time.

Father did not go back to New Mexico. They did go on a honeymoon, to Sweet Springs, West Virginia in the valley, where they had dear friends. 1917 was an unsettling year in world events. [The last Russian czar abdicated and Lenin brought his new brand of politics to Moscow. President Wilson declared war on Germany April 2. Germany bombed London June 13. And, Susie and Calvin Satterfield's son, Calvin Jr, went off to war.]

* * *

A very special day for the Satterfield family and the Chalfonte was July 3, 1999, when Phoebe

SPECIAL DAY
Above: Amanda Sullivan on her wedding day at the Chalfonte with husband Gary Bernstein and Brenda Bartella Peterson, who married them. Right: Amanda arriving via the fire escape.
Amanda Sullivan

A Matrimonial Milestone

Excerpt from The Chalfonte Newsletter, Spring, 1998...

The setting was perfect for the September 1997 wedding of Amanda Sullivan and Gary Bernstein. It wasn't just a wedding. It was an all-out three-day celebration attended by more than 100 friends and family, many of whom have been guests (and staff) at the hotel for decades.

The story begins when Amanda's parents, Robert (Sully) Sullivan and the late Merrinelle Rice Sullivan met at the Chalfonte in 1957. They married in 1960, returning each year, eventually with daughters Amanda and Susan in tow. Amanda grew up at the hotel and worked there for many years. The guests and staff became her extended family.

After meeting Gary Bernstein in Chicago, the couple eventually made their way to Amanda's hometown of New York. Sometime between their first meeting and their wedding day, a marriage proposal was accepted in the hotel's cupola.

With lifelong memories of the Chalfonte, the couple thoughtfully incorporated the hotel's culture, history, ambiance (and Dot and Lucille's specialties) into every aspect of the weekend, from rehearsal dinner to ceremony to reception.

After the ceremony, Amanda recalls how she and Gary walked through the crowd of family and friends, into the arms of chefs Dot and Lucille, who have known Amanda since birth. "It couldn't have been more perfect. They're my family!"

Satterfield Peyton's great-granddaughter also chose the Chalfonte for her wedding reception. Mary Peyton Lynch and Travis Roy Worthington said their vows at St Peter's-by-the-Sea at Cape May Point and rode by horse and carriage to the Chalfonte, once owned by the bride's great-great grandparents.

Mary Peyton Lynch Worthington *Oakland, California* "When we arrived at the hotel we were greeted by 90 or so guests [many Satterfield relatives were in attendance] who were all jubilant, with Dot and Lucille's wonderful southern cooking having its comfort effect. There's nothing better than Dot and Lucille's crab cakes for appetizers at your wedding! Then on to the seafood bisque, poached salmon, filet mignon, Chalfonte green beans, oven roasted potatoes, champagne and wedding cake!

"Grandmother Phoebe Peyton was unable to be there; she was caring for my grandfather in San Antonio. In a note she wrote, 'I wish you both the happiest of marriages. You seem made for each other, a truly beautiful couple. All my love, Grandma.'

"And a happy life we have had. We celebrated our 10th wedding anniversary last year. We have two lovely boys: Thomas Taft Worthington and Peyton James Worthington. I couldn't have imagined a more perfect place to spend my wedding day. There is such warmth and charm to the beautiful old Chalfonte, and such wonderful memories that go far back for me and my whole family. We would get together one July week every third summer to reunite and be taken into the bosom of the old walls, the porch rockers and each other's company. We'd share old photographs, family stories and history, relax at the beach and end each day with a wonderful meal together in the grand dining room."

Cricket & Pat Satterfield *Richmond, Virginia* [Pat] "We were staying at the Howard Street Cottage for a weekend, I believe celebrating Cricket's March 11th birthday. It was Sunday. The church bells were ringing on a beautiful spring morning. I looked out the window and saw a wedding in progress on the widow's walk

TRADITION CONTINUES
Phoebe's great-grand daughter Mary Peyton Lynch chose the Chalfonte for her wedding to Travis Worthington July 3, 1999. The Satterfield family gathered for the celebration.
Phoebe Peyton Hanson

The CHALFONTE

of the Abbey. The bells are ringing and I said, 'Sounds like wedding bells to me. And, Cricket said, 'Let's get married, and let's get married here.'

"We began planning a September wedding, 1988, at the willow tree. We borrowed a handmade tent from Curtis Bashaw, whose grandfather, the Reverend Carl McIntire, had preached under the tent in Pakistan and shipped it home for use here at his Cape May hotels. Cricket wore a white linen suit like his grandfather used to wear. Anne LeDuc caught my bouquet. She nonchalantly hung on the sidelines until the moment, and then pounced in one of her hockey moves and won the toss."

Amanda Sullivan *New York City* "When my boyfriend, Gary Bernstein, visited the Chalfonte, we decided that like my parents, we would become engaged at the hotel. We picked out a ring on the Washington Street Mall. I asked Gary if we could go to the cupola for the proposal. What a romantic spot. We had a Tin House wedding on September 23, 1997. Our son Henry, born in 2000, is named for Henry Sawyer, builder of the hotel, and Henry, the legend-

CHALFONTE CAST
Bill Fralin met his wife Kate when they were staffers. When they married October 15, 1988, many of the guests were Chalfonte friends. They return to the hotel annually for summer fun with their children.
Fralin family collection

PAKISTANI STYLE
Opposite: Old family customs of Ali Naqvi, originally of Pakistan, were part of the festivities of his marriage to Linda Holliday Labor Day weekend 2005. The couple, like so many before them, married at the Tin House and had their reception in the Magnolia Room and on the porches. They return to the hotel for extended family reunions.
Naqvi-Holliday family collection

ary bellhop. Our twins Bobby and Simone, born in 2005, were honored at a celebration of life ceremony at the Tin House. Judy Bartella's stepmother, Brenda Bartella Peterson, an ordained minister, presided at both our life celebration and wedding ceremony."

* * *

Ali Naqvi of Lahur, Pakistan and Linda Holliday of Detroit, Michigan, met while attending the Wharton School of the University of Pennsylvania in Philadelphia. When they decided to marry Labor Day weekend, 2005, they chose the Chalfonte because it was like a family home, "like grandmother's house," said Linda. Ali had vacationed here with his daughters in 2001 when Alizay was nine and Shahav five. "It was a sanctuary," said Ali. "It provided a lovely peace."

"We come from very different cultures, Linda and I," said Ali. "We wanted a place for our families to get to know each other, to be able to sit and visit. We wanted a coming together of our families before the ceremony."

Linda Holliday "I did not want our wedding day to be one of introducing strangers. Our guests came to the hotel on Friday, and they

232

had the luxury of meeting each other. We could have had our wedding in New York, but I wanted the place to be real, to be authentic. I don't like a contrived, pretentious setting. Our wedding was lovely. We had a barbecue and dancing out back on Friday night, cocktails and guitar music on the porch and our ceremony at the willow tree under a canopy. A wonderful reception followed in the Magnolia Room, decorated with tiny twinkle lights and white, yellow and blue meadow flowers."

Ali Naqvi "For me, this place is déjà vu. In Pakistan, my city, Lahur, is a historic city, a Colonial city. There are buildings similar to the Chalfonte, built in the same period, the Edwardian period. The British built summer retreats, hill stations, similar to this, so the Chalfonte is very familiar to me. This place is not just a building, it is like a fine old painting. And the owner is a custodian of this fine piece of art. We feel privileged to participate, and return here where we were married with our extended families. They look forward to it. There is no tight schedule. My daughters bring their friends. My mother is here, Linda's relatives are here. There can be a late breakfast, tea on the porch in the afternoon. It's Grandmother's house."

Bill & Kate Fralin *Washington, DC* [Bill] "John Grove whose mother and father fell in love at the Chalfonte, and his great-aunt Grovie worked here, said, 'I know a place, a summer place, where for work you get room and board. There's a beach and a lot of young people and it's great fun. Are you interested?'

"'Absolutely,' I said.

"John said, 'It's in New Jersey.'

"I said, 'New Jersey, why do I need to go to New Jersey? My mother is from Lewes, Delaware and we never crossed the bay.' All I knew of New Jersey was the industrial wasteland along the northern stretch of the Parkway. John is my friend, so I came along, and I was charmed right away by this charming Victorian village and the Chalfonte. I fell in love with the Chalfonte from the moment I saw it. I worked a while that first year in 1982. In 83 I came back with a group of

ROMANTIC SETTING
Tlhe Chalfonte's lacy old Valentine appearance makes it a special wedding site. Stacy Johnson and Brian Firlein and their party at the entrance to the Magnolia Room July 20, 2010.
Photograph by Andres Valenzuela Photography
andresvalenzuela.com

guys from UVA for pre-season cleanup.

"Eight of us guys are sitting on the porch, and a car pulls up and a beautiful blonde emerges. Now she's facing off with eight guys, and we all say, this one is for me. One of the guys makes fast tracks, buys her flowers, takes her to dinner. They become a couple and Kate and I become friends, but we are both dating other people. And that's the way it went for a couple years until I graduated from college and our friendship turned into a romance. We were married October 15th, 1988, with a cast of Chalfonte friends at the wedding. I have returned to Cape May every single summer since that first summer in 1982. Sometimes it's just a long weekend at the hotel. This summer of 2010 I'm here for two weeks with my family, Kate, myself and our three children Abby, 15, who is thinking about working here one day, my son Hayden, 13, and Hallie, 9, named for a Cape May friend Hallie Boyce who was in our wedding.

"Let me say that without Anne LeDuc this place would be a Howard Johnson's. She saved this wonderful building and way of life. Her business partner Judy Bartella made the trains run on time. Anne has this way about her. She not only embodied the Chalfonte, but embedded

From The Archives

Excerpt from The Chalfonte Newsletter, 1987...

Two Dickerson family weddings at the hotel were highlights for 1986. Dot's daughter Tina (named for her great-grandmother Clementine who worked at the hotel as head chambermaid for 60 years) was married at the Tin House in June. Lucille's son Chuckie had his wedding reception at the hotel in October. Congratulations!

CHALFONTE MAGIC

With Cape May one of the top wedding destinations in the country, the new owners, the Mullocks, have focused on the wedding business. Bob and Linda Mullock understand the Chalfonte magic. They were married there 30 years ago. Wedding coordinator Terry Carr facilitated more than 20 weddings at the hotel in 2010 and has bookings for 2011 and 2012.

it into all of us college youngsters who worked here. We'd come in after a night of hell raisin', and Anne would leave one of those notes of hers. 'Staff: Two guests checked out because of the noise.' Then later in the day, we were called in for a talking-to. She had a way of making your head hang low, she never overdid it; then would move on, and held no grudges and it was a new day. She balanced a lot of worlds. When I came here Mrs S. [Satterfield] and Mrs N. [Nash] were still here. And it was imperative to pay tribute to them in the lobby. Anne had the ability to bring in a new generation with her innate people skills. Without Anne, the passing of generations would not have occurred.

"Anne has kept up with hundreds of people who have worked here. She not only keeps up with those of us who were on staff, she keeps up with our families and intimately knows what's going on. Chalfonte staffs, and hundreds of Chalfonte guests, are Anne's family. A remarkable person."

John Grove's parents fell in love at the Chalfonte in the 1950s. John grew up at the hotel in summers, and worked there several seasons while in college. When news of John's engagement to Kate Bateman hit the Chalfonte, no

time was wasted planning for a big party in their honor at the Tin House. The party, on July 8, 2006, drew a guest list of family, friends and members of the Chalfonte staff who have known John Grove and his mother Margaret for many seasons.

Lou and Linda Riccio *Malvern, Pennsylvania, and West Cape May* [Lou] "I was in Cape May for a wedding in 1987, staying at a house rented by my ex-brother-in-law. The phone rang and this woman called – actually it was her house, which she had sublet, in which I was staying. She said she was at the ferry landing and needed a ride to Cape May. I said, 'Well sure, I'll pick you up.'

"The woman is Linda and we drive back to Cape May and our conversation is easy right away. We went to dinner that night at the Mad Batter and I became very engaged as to who Linda was as a person. She said let's go for a drink at the King Eddie at the Chalfonte, and it is there that I start to meet all of these characters with whom Linda worked at the hotel. On subsequent visits I met the kitchen staff and Linda's hero, Helen, the cook, and her daughters Dot and Ceilly.

"When I asked Linda to marry me, I not only had to ask her father but also Miss Helen, who

ENGAGEMENT PARTY
Opposite, left: John Grove, a Chalfonte boy of summer, introduced fiancée Kate at a 2006 Tin House party.
John Grove

STAFFER WEDS
Opposite, right: Jean Lloyd (dancing with her father) chose a Chalfonte reception after her wedding to John Larson in 1990.

KING EDDIE CONNECTION
Above, left: Longtime staffer Linda Buchanan and Lou Riccio married in Pittsburgh, but many of their guests were hotel friends.

CHALFONTE BABY
Above, right: Linda Riccio continued working at the hotel when her son Michael was a baby. The staff enjoyed being part of Michael's day care.
Riccio family collection

considered Linda her princess. We were married in 1989. In 1990, when our son Michael was born, Linda still wanted to work at the Chalfonte. I came down on the weekends to be with her and the baby. We lived in the Tin House or in Theodore's tiny room off the Sawyer Room. Linda worked and the staff helped care for Michael. At night when we went to the King Eddie for a nightcap, we'd sometimes wheeled in Michael right beside us. It was a great experience with him in the Tin House. We'd hear the horse and carriage sounds of the clopping along Sewell Avenue and the ocean in the distance. Linda has had every job at the Chalfonte over 30 years from chambermaid to dining room hostess. Our son, the Chalfonte baby, worked as a bus boy recently before he went off to Haverford College."

The CHALFONTE

HOW SWEET
Angela and Mike Post sharing
a wedding kiss while their
carriage awaits.
Photograph by KGM Expressions
kgmexpressions.com

CHAPTER XII

Old Meets New: The Mullock Mission

HE old Chalfonte is nothing new to the hotel's latest owner, Bob Mullock and his family. He and his wife Linda were married at the hotel in 1981. Bob and Linda were among the renaissance couples who found their way to Cape May in the late 70s and invested their savings, blood, sweat and tears in restoring and converting worn-out Victorian houses into charming B&Bs. Bob was a successful financial manager during his corporate days and, like previous Chalfonte owners, has a diverse history of his own.

"Linda and I had been dating and one day as the weekend approached, Linda said, 'I'd like to take you out for a weekend.' She picked me up and drove me to a place I had never been before, Cape May. She pulled up by the Mainstay, Tom and Sue Carroll's recently restored beautiful B&B. I bought champagne for dinner and a seafood sampler for the beach. We walked around looking at the architecture and I thought, this is a great place. When we walked down Columbia Avenue past the Southern Inn, it was in bad

"That time in Cape May was one of the best times of my life. Linda and I had fallen in love. The work ethic among the B&B couples was extraordinary. Some of us had corporate positions, and on the weekends we traveled to Cape May and spent 12-14 hours a day renovating, spackling, painting. There wasn't a lot of nightlife in those days."

shape and for sale. This is before the big influx, as the B&B industry was just getting started. Linda said, 'I have always wanted a B&B.' Now I'm about 30 at the time, and I said, 'Well, why don't I just call, and maybe I will invest with you, and we can come down on weekends and fix up this place.'

Bob and Linda purchased the Southern Inn and spent the winter giving rebirth to the 1872 Gothic revival. By the next season it was a pretty B&B called the Victorian Rose with a garden out front featuring roses big as teacups that bloomed until Christmas. Linda nurtured the Victorian Rose to success with her sweet personality, subtle humor and an expert culinary hand at breakfasts and tea time, while Bob continued his business career.

The business of operating an inn or hotel comes naturally for Linda. Her family, the Kelleys, ran a small hotel in Ocean City, Maryland after settling on an Eastern Shore farm in the early 1800s. After serving in the US Navy in World War II, Linda's father, Everett Kelley, and wife Ellie established a professional placement firm, Everett Kelley Associates in Philadelphia. The business continues today in a second generation.

"That time in Cape May was one of the best times of my life," says Bob. "Linda and I had fallen in love. The work ethic among the B&B couples was extraordinary. Some of us had corporate positions, and on the weekends we traveled to Cape May and spent 12-14 hours a day renovating, spackling, painting. There wasn't a lot of nightlife in those days. On winter evenings, the streets were dark, and only a few people were out and about. We did party and the dress was paint pants, old T-shirts and sweatshirts, bandanas and heavy tattoos of paint and spackle."

The Victorian Rose was just steps from the Chalfonte compound. Bob became a regular around the hotel, with alley privileges to the kitchen where the cooks, Helen and her daughters, Dot and Lucille, were preparing their fried chicken and yeast rolls. He loved the fried chicken and downhome goodness of the food. "The hotel fascinated me," he says, "not only the architecture, but its history and warm hospitable feel."

Bob and Chalfonte owner Anne LeDuc became good friends. They shared some of the same views about humanitarian efforts in faraway places. And they exchanged ideas about

Cape May's growing popularity and the hospitality industry.

Anne and Judy Bartella purchased the Chalfonte in 1982. About the same time, Bob Mullock was growing weary of catching the 5:59 dirty diesel train from Philadelphia, joining his wife in the evenings at the Victorian Rose. Bob had established a career in Philadelphia as a marketing and planning vice president for INA and Cigna Corporation and decided to take a risk. He left his lucrative corporate position and moved to the shore full-time. He joined National Associates Insurance of Cape May, specializing in planning and expansion, and became a partner.

Life was good. The Mullocks were expecting their first child, Zachary, in 1985. Bob grew up in Bucks County, Pennsylvania when it was still open woods and farmland and he wanted open

CHALFONTE WEDDING
Linda and Bob Mullock have loved the hotel for a long time. They had their wedding at the hotel in 1981. The couple is pictured with daughter Cynthia and the kitchen staff.

NEW OWNERS
Opposite: Linda and Bob Mullock and family decided to buy the venerable Chalfonte in 2008. They have years of experience in business and hospitality. Linda's family, the Kelleys, settled in Maryland in the early 1800s and operated a small hotel in Ocean City.
Mullock family collection

space for his children. He and Linda moved to Cape May Point near the beach, Lake Lily and the lighthouse, where there is hardly any traffic in the off-season. Youngsters ride their bikes everywhere and play hockey in the streets. As the family grew, this was the perfect scenario. They welcomed son Dillon in 1987 and daughter Ellie in 1991. Cynthia, Bob's older daughter from a previous marriage, joined them every summer.

Bob remembers he got his first summer job at age 12. He hitch-hiked to the Warrington Golf Club and caddied 18 holes for $4. He was the fourth in a family of nine children, seven boys and two girls. He's from a coal miner's family that settled in Minersville, a rough and tumble Pennsylvania town.

"Grandfather left the farm and the horrors of the Russian Revolution and World War I in 1918.

He and his family emigrated through Austria in 1918 to the safety of America. The family grew to 10. Grandfather was tough. He became the sheriff, fought the circus boxer and won, and lost his leg in a coal mining accident. He saw three of his sons off to World War II – one to Pearl Harbor, another to the Atlantic Navy. My father Norman was in the Air Force, a navigator on a B-17. He flew more than 25 bombing missions over Germany. He lost many friends. My mother's father loaded ships in wartime London.

"During the bombing her family moved her to safety in the country. Margaret Rose Clark was Dad's British war bride. After returning from the war, Dad's perfect world was to buy a four-bedroom rancher in the suburbs for his nine children, with an in-ground swimming pool and good schools. He became a plastics engineer. He died at age 44, leaving a lot of little ones for Mom to raise. I was in college, and older. I helped her however and whenever I could. I worked my way through college. I never asked for money because there was none."

After caddying for years, Bob knew a lot about golf and golf courses. In 1988 he learned that a 150-acre farm just outside Cape May was going into development for 150 houses. Bob, a proponent of preserving historical landmarks and open space, decided to save the landscape.

"This was one of the only large tracts of farmland left in the area. It had some important ecological value for birds and other wildlife and geographic rarity. It lay next to saltwater wetlands and within a few feet had natural fresh water. It was the perfect spot for a golf course."

Designed by Bob and landscape architect Karl Litten, one of the best golf course planners in the world, the Cape May National Golf Course opened in 1991. The flat farm had been sculpted into a gently rolling 18-hole course. Golf writers nicknamed it 'The Natural' and that fit Bob Mullock's vision to a tee. The course features expanded wetlands, seven lakes and ponds, 1,500 additional trees, a variety of grasses. It serves not only as a golf course but a 50-acre bird sanctuary. Water is captured and recycled for irrigation and a new solar system will make the course a self-sustaining environment.

Bob was at the top of his game. His golf course was an immediate success and his insurance partnership was doing well. Just as the course was completed, Bob was reading *The New York Times* one morning. He had been horrified that week by images on television showing the

VICTORIAN ROSE BED & BREAKFAST ❧ CAPE MAY.

After caddying for years, Bob knew a lot about golf and golf courses. In 1988 he learned that a 150-acre farm just outside Cape May was going into development for 150 houses. Bob, a proponent of preserving historical landmarks and open space, decided to save the landscape.

starving in Somalia, caught in famine and civil war, among feuding clans and their militias. Somalia had fallen into anarchy after the long-term president was overthrown.

"This one sentence got me thinking. It said the New York office of the Somalia Mission to the United Nations had no office supplies. How could that be? I picked up the phone and called. The woman said they had one broken typewriter and a stapler. I gathered some office supplies from National Associates and drove to New York. I confirmed what I read. There were four staffers in the office, unpaid volunteers, and a broken typewriter and a stapler. I met the Somalia UN Ambassador Fatun Hassan who painted a picture worse than TV – of children dying at the rate several a day at the refugee orphanage in Baidoa."

This is the sort of story about which movies are made. Bob Mullock decided he was going to the front lines. With Linda and his elementary school age boys Zachary and Dillon helping, he packed a GI duffle bag with medical supplies, old clothing and a dozen Frisbees on top. Linda tucked in a couple jars of peanut butter. Bob caught a plane to Nairobi, Kenya, and hitchhiked by plane and truck 250 miles into Somalia.

"The Nairobi newspaper the day I arrived described the town of Baidoa as the 'city of

death', with an average of 150 people dying daily, 6,000 last month alone. If I'm here to help, I may as well work with the people who need help more than anyone else – the children."

Mullock purchased supplies for his incursion into Baidoa. He had no military or State Department clearance. He was a one-man relief mission with $5,000 in cash, most of which he hid between two pieces of wood in a Nairobi hotel room drawer until a later return visit for supplies. He searched the streets in the city, gathering supplies transportable by taxi to the airport. He had no reservations. He knew no one.

"I realize at this point everything I have is in my bags. It's amazing how many things we think we need to function and how things can be

THIS IS THE PLACE
Bob Mullock and Linda when they first bought the Southern Inn on Columbia Avenue, steps from the Chalfonte, and transformed it into the Victorian Rose (pictured on opposite page).
Mullock family collection

pared down to no more than what fits into two duffle bags when circumstances require it."

Bob negotiated a ride on a mail flight from Mogadishu to Baidoa. Like Civil War hero Henry Sawyer, the first owner of the Chalfonte who wrote a diary of war and imprisonment, Bob kept a diary of his risky mission.

"Looking out the plane window I notice the red, dusty earth is barren. The houses below look as though they have been bombed out. None have roofs. Our landing field is nothing more than a 50-foot wide strip. There is no tarmac, no control tower, no runway lights. The plane never really stops. The pilots are anxious to get out of there. They throw my duffle bags off the back and hand me a bundle of letters. 'Here's the mail. Good luck.'

"By the time I notice the armed rebels creeping out of the bushes surrounding the landing strip, the plane has become nothing more than a speck in the sky. I wish I had a gun. The rebel leader moves out of the pack. Rough, hardened by time in the bush and the experience of war… he is six-foot-tall, thin but sinewy… He smells the air. I am no threat. To show him I come with good intentions, I pull a pair of pants and a T-shirt out of my bags to give as a peace offering. He appears happy with the gift and passes the clothing to one of his men.

"Baidoa is teeming with people, all of them starving. They are gaunt-faced, leaning over, using whatever they can find to support their bodies. Looking at them, I feel I have been dropped into a concentration camp. There are bundles of rags in the weeds and huddled into balls along the road. I am struck by the sudden realization that each ball is a child huddling against the trembles of weakness, sickness, starving alone amongst a mass of desperate people suffering in the heat.

"I learn that Baidoa is an oasis in this desert. The people in surrounding villages stay in their homes to wait out the famine until they are consumed by hunger and then walk to Baidoa in search of food. The people I see crowding the streets have walked for miles in their starvation, arriving in the city, their last hope on their baked feet. I am no longer worried about being a crazy American wondering whether I can be useful. Where do I start? The main orphanage building is one-story masonry, but the windows are fashioned from broken slats and there is no roof, forcing children to huddle together on cool nights and there is no protection from rain. Some children are clothed, others are naked, nearly all of them are extremely thin and sickly."

Bob teamed up with Mohaumoud Iman Aden, the well respected leader, translator and peace negotiator, and founder of the Baidoa orphanage. For the next month Bob used his military and corporate skills to shuttle supplies from Nairobi to Baidoa, providing food, medicine, clothing, tools, cups, bowls and materials for a roof. He negotiated trips on American C130s that were dropping grain shipments for the starving before US Marines arrived.

He made several trips to Baidoa, raising money – a lot of it in Cape May through his friend and business partner Charlie Pessagno – to build structures for 1,500 children who within

From The Archives

▨ Bob Mullock graduated from Central Bucks High School, Doylestown, Pennsylvania in 1967. He studied political science at Indiana University of Pennsylvania and was student body president at a time of student, civil rights and Vietnam war unrest. He worked both sides of the street, so to speak, coming to terms with campus issues, becoming the first student on the university board of trustees, and instrumental in the university becoming one of the first college in the nation having student representation in the college senate.

When Black Panther members from Pittsburgh took over the college radio station, authorities asked Mullock to negotiate. He told the Panthers that law enforcement officials were going to take the station back and there was no negotiating that fact. The Panthers gave back the microphone and vacated the station without incident. Mullock was in ROTC and after graduation trained in the Army for Vietnam. He was six weeks into eight week training in helicopters, ammunition and jungle warfare when the Colonel walked in and said President Nixon was bringing home troops. He went on to serve as a captain in the reserves until 1975.

Mullock has degrees in finance and business from Temple University and the University of Pennsylvania.

a year were not only being fed and doctored, but who were attending school. He worked with the locals to reestablish a 90-acre farm and populate it with 40 oxen and chickens. He provided seeds for a garden. Three wells were dug. A vocational training school trained students in weaving and sewing.

The Baidoa orphanage was possibly the most positive story in Somalia. As George H. W. Bush's presidency wound down, 20,000 Marines transported food to ease the famine and the president visited the orphanage in January 1992. Fledgling UN peace talks were held at the orphanage, called the Cape May School, in August, 1993.

Bob says he carried peace proposals from Somali General Mohammed Farrah Aideed to the US State Department in Washington, and helped arrange a meeting between Presidential Special US Ambassador Robert Oakley and warring militia leaders at Baidoa.

Soon after, peace and humanitarian efforts collapsed as warlords seized food shipments and claimed them as their own. Somalia fell into anarchy as evidenced in the October, 1993 Black Hawk Down incident. General Aideed was a target of the US Special Forces operation in Mogadishu, resulting in street militas shooting down two Black Hawk choppers. Eighteen Americans were killed, 73 wounded. Television audiences were horrified seeing US troops, dead and wounded, dragged through the streets.

Seriously wounded pilot Mike Durant was taken prisoner and Bob says the State Department asked him to appeal to General Aideed for Durant's release. He did so and credits Ambas-

NEW YORK   BAIDOA

'They're just like my children,' says N.J. volunteer in Somalia

The Associated Press

A step ahead of the cavalry, Robert Mullock pressed his own Operation Restore Hope on Tuesday, handing Christmas to cheering orphans he is helping to save.

No one seems to mind that the kids are mostly Muslims.

"I have four of my own," Mullock said. "When I saw these kids with the same mannerisms, like pulling at my face, I realized there was no difference. These children, they're just like my children."

Until September, he watched the piteous images on TV and shook his head like everyone else. Then, in the newspaper, he read that Somalia's U.N. mission didn't even have a working typewriter.

"They couldn't even make their plea to the world," the 43-year-old insurance man said. "Here, I thought, is at least something I can do to help."

He drove to New York from his home in Cape May. Sure enough, only the stapler worked at the Somali mission. He raised money for a bank of memory typewriters and other essentials.

"From these people, I got a different angle on Somalis," Mullock said. "I had thought they were mean and awful and always killing each other. They are very nice people."

That was when he jumped in with both feet.

His family helped pack a bag. His partners at the National Group insurance agency took over his work. He flew to Nairobi, Kenya, and hitched a ride to Baidoa, where he met Mohamoud Imam Aden.

"This is the saint of Somalia," he said, with a fond hand on Iman Aden's shoulder. Mullock threw his energies behind his friend's orphanage for 600 boys, aged 2 to 14. The orphanage feeds and clothes 1,200 more.

On that first trip, he counted nine bodies from the airport into town. He had only a bag of sugar to give away, and he handed it to a small boy.

"He took it in the bushes and looked around and then opened it," Mullock said. Demonstrating with his index finger and tongue, he added, "He ate it, grain by grain, until he finished the bag."

When he found the orphanage had no medicine, he hopped an empty relief flight to Mombasa, Kenya. Passing himself of as a doctor, he brought back full cartons.

Back in New Jersey, Mullock raised $30,000. He returned last week with 1,500 sheets of metal roofing and to see what more he could do.

He saw that well over half the "gunmen" who terrorized S malia are youngsters who should be in class.

"We've got to get the guns out of these kids' hands and get them in school," Mullock said.

BAIDOA ORPHANAGE
Top left: Happy youngsters in school after Bob Mullock helped restore the orphanage, home to famine-stricken children.

NATIONAL EXPOSURE
Top right: Bob Mullock describing the Baidoa orphanage project to Katie Couric on the NBC *Today* show – his story was also featured in newspapers. Bob arrived in Somalia and began his relief mission before the US Marines arrived to airlift food and medicine.

THE TEAM
Above left: Mullock pictured with Baidoa locals and officials who joined in a team to rebuild the war-torn orphanage and farm in 1991-92.

IN SOMALIA
Left: Writing his journal aboard an American cargo plane en route to the orphanage. Mullock became known as Dr Bob for transporting medical supplies to starving orphans.

Mullock family collection

sador Oakley for negotiating the pilot's freedom in 11 days. Later, at Aideed's invitation, Bob returned to retrieve Durant's personal possessions. On his return home, he was debriefed by government officials. By then, it was impossible to sustain humanitarian efforts in Somalia.

Bob says he came back from Somalia a changed person. He learned to live on bare essentials, without phones, television, computers. He says he felt detoxed from technology. He and Linda made a decision to have no television in their home for the next 10 years, even though they had three youngsters. They watched important sports events and school assignments on the TV at the golf course.

Bob continued work in Kenya through 2003, and with Somalia out of reach, the Mullock family found new destinations for humanitarian projects. Together Bob and Linda traveled to The Farm of the Child, a New Jersey group's effort in Honduras. Linda measured orphans and staff for shoes, and funds were donated for a medical clinic.

The family was proud of daughter Cynthia when she initiated "Starvation Day" at her high school on Martin Luther King Day, with students donating their lunch money to children in Somalia. When she appeared on the *Today* show from Abington High School, Pennsylvania to talk about her project, other schools around the country instituted an annual day of hunger. Cynthia went on to teach English in Chile and open an internet café in Santiago. Bob, Zachary and Dillon traveled to Chile and Ecuador, witnessing poverty among children their own age. Orphans took Zachary into the jungle to show how they hunted iguana with a spear to obtain their rare source of meat. When Bob heard the story he found a grill and served the children hamburgers and ice cream, treats most had never enjoyed.

Their most recent effort was in Haiti where Bob and younger daughter Ellie traveled to support a local church project. Arriving at the airport where men stood armed with shotguns was a culture shock to 17- year-old Ellie, but she was able to see the house they sponsored and its importance to Haitian families.

In 2006, Bob ran for Congress as an Independent against veteran Republican Frank LoBiondo. He knew it was a long shot, but he had some issues he wanted to address. He thought the war in Iraq was foolish, was against privatizing Social Security, worried about the loss of

ALL SMILES
Opposite, top: Meet the Chalfonte staff, pictured from left, Megan Gillen-Schwartz, Trace and Jackie Brown (volunteers), Dillon Mullock, Terry Carr, LuAnn Daniels and Nancy Granick.
Photo by Aleksey Moryakov

HOCKEY STARS
Opposite, below: Zach and Dillon Mullock started playing hockey at their Cape May Point home. Both excelled at hockey at Mount St Mary's University.
Mullock family collection

American jobs and the middle class and felt lobbyists were buying Congress. "I knew it was a quixotic effort, but the issues were so important and at that time there was little debate on these issues by the major parties."

It was after a campaign speech at the VFW in West Cape May that negotiations began regarding the Chalfonte. "I was pleased to see that Anne LeDuc was kind to come and support me. She had supported me in many projects over the years, especially involving orphanages. I was expecting her to say – Bob, great speech. But she also wanted to talk about the sale of the Chalfonte. I said, 'I didn't know it was for sale.'

"She said, 'Everyone in town knows it – well, it is for sale.' The next day the talks began. It was a long dance. In the end, my family voted on the purchase. It was close, but the vote was yes. The documents were signed July 1, 2008. It was important to have the entire family support the purchase. We prayed together about the decision. I knew if the family owned the hotel, we had to commit to long-term preservation, which would involve the next generation, our children."

Linda is the centerpiece of this remarkable family. She is always there for counsel and support for her husband, adult children and the Chalfonte staff. Twenty years running the Victorian Rose B&B gave her valuable experience in hospitality, plus she is an accomplished cook and decorator. Linda has added tasteful comfort and color to the Chalfonte with her flower arrangements and restyled rooms, carefully leaving intact the historic integrity. And she's added special desserts to the Magnolia Room menu; her chocolate pie the most popular.

The Chalfonte Mullock Mission is, indeed, a family venture. Daughter Cynthia served as a financial advisor in the purchase of the hotel. She has a joint law and masters of business degree from Columbia University, is fluent in French and Spanish, and serves as vice president of a Princeton, New Jersey investment firm. Sons Zachary and Dillon graduated from Mt Saint Mary's University. Both played college ice hockey and golf. Zachary was class president and Dillon was captain of the ice hockey team. Daughter Ellie is studying to be a nurse.

The family divides responsibilities, with Dillon and mother Linda hands-on at the hotel. Dillon started working at the Chalfonte the summer before his senior year in college, learning Magnolia Room and front desk procedures. He has been promoted to operations manager

and enjoys spending time with guests to ensure their time here is enjoyable.

Zachary has assumed more operational duties at the golf course, while Bob Mullock works in both worlds. He is president of the Chalfonte, but mingles with guests and loves telling the North-South Civil War stories of Henry Sawyer and Susie Satterfield. He manages without a cell phone and with minimum time at a computer. He doesn't get "hit with a fire hose of technology," as he puts it, cluttering his head and hampering his vision; something he learned in Somalia. He runs his businesses from a small office at the golf course.

Anne LeDuc and Judy Bartella's goal in selling the hotel was to guarantee that Cape May's Grande Dame would not meet a fatal fate. They wanted to assure she would not be gutted and converted into condominiums; its auxiliary buildings and grounds turned into yet another parking lot. They took less for the property, as the Satterfields did, to satisfy a long-term stewardship of the oldest hotel in Cape May.

GOOD LUCK
Hughes Street neighbor Michael Longfellow says it was an unusual weather day when he went chasing a rainbow, and snapped this photograph as the colors arched over the Grande Dame of Cape May.

"I have great respect for Anne and Judy," says Bob. "They maintained the Chalfonte through the most trying financial times and never sold out. There is something very communal about the Chalfonte, and it is a richness they encouraged. Although now in her 80s, Anne's devotion to the hotel continues. I treasure her wisdom and while we sometimes tangle over the details, I love her give and take. She has such mettle and spirit; I look forward to our engagements."

Bob's intention in purchasing the Chalfonte was to preserve the traditions and historic quality of the building and its environment. He understood there would be a major investment of time and money in its preservation, which his philosophy allows.

"I am not interested in being rich. I want to live an enriched life. At the peak of the real estate bubble, three of the largest real estate firms in the country flew planes over our golf course. They sent drawings of mansions – all sorts of different types of dwellings – and designs to be situated on our golf course for untold millions of dollars. I am not interested in that. Nor am I interested in converting the Chalfonte into 25 condos at half a million each. I didn't choose the Chalfonte, the Chalfonte chose us."

The family paid nearly three million dollars for the Chalfonte compound. Another million was invested in 34 first-time private baths, new plumbing, electric, air conditioning, fire alarms and a fire suppression system. Bob says he knew that if the Chalfonte closed during the summer season, it might never reopen, and so the massive, complex project needed to be completed in six months. Local general contractor Ken Mann brought in workers during holidays, weekends and nights to meet the deadline. Rather than tear up the place and remove ancient wires and pipes, the Mullocks decided to tie off the old conduits and leave them be. The new were installed in specially designed soffits and arches that are noticeable only if pointed out.

Redoing plumbing in a 134-year-old building was a puzzle. Bob was advised to cut the number of bedrooms in half to make room for new baths. Instead he designed bathrooms inspired by compact baths he experienced in Europe. Only two guest rooms were lost in the redesign and four suites were created using storage space. In-room sinks were repaired and new plumbing installed. Where once the hotel's entire water supply had to be shut off for one leaking faucet, now each fixture has its own hot and cold water lines.

Renovations began after Christmas 2008 and as Memorial Day 2009 approached the old hotel bustled around the clock. Custom headboards created by a Florida firm were driven to Cape May by the designer-owner himself to make sure they fit the new mattresses and bed frames. The Chalfonte's antique furniture was polished and placed in freshly painted rooms. The large original Chalfonte sign, long ago broken, was recreated by local artist Emilie Randolph and placed in its traditional spot below the cupola and lit up at night. "The place buzzed like a movie set," said Megan Gillen-Schwartz, project manager, as the doors were opened for a new season, welcoming guests old and new.

An important milestone in the Mullocks' mission was the Chalfonte's selection in 2010 as one of the Historic Hotels of America in the National Trust for Historic Preservation. More than 220 hotels are on the list for having faithfully maintained their historic architecture and ambiance. To be selected the hotel must meet a list of criteria, including being at least 50 years old, listed in or eligible for the National Register of Historic Places, or recognized locally as having historic significance. This selection will open the Chalfonte to a new clientele interested in experiencing living and dining in an authentic American treasure.

The Mullocks continue to design a maintenance and business plan with the goal of preserving the Chalfonte for at least 50 more years.

The year 2011 is a significant one for the Chalfonte families: the Sawyer and Satterfield descendants, the Mullocks and former owners Anne LeDuc and Judy Bartella, who worked so hard for so many years to maintain the hotel and its lifestyle. It is the Chalfonte's 135 birthday. The year also marks the 100th anniversary of Susie and Calvin Satterfield opening the hotel under their management in 1911. And it's the 150th anniversary of the Civil War in which the Sawyer, Satterfield and LeDuc families participated in the conflict, from both sides.

At the Chalfonte, the North and South come together culturally, geographically and historically. The Mullocks are determined to preserve and protect that legacy.

MAGICAL MOMENT
Salty ocean breezes waft in from the Atlantic Ocean, while guests relax on the rockers.
Photograph by John Lynner Peterson

The old lady relaxes in the off-season and is ready, once again, to throw open her doors to the people who have grown to love her.
Photograph by John Lynner Peterson
johnlynnerpeterson.com

About The Author

Karen Fox spent most of her career in a television newsroom as an editor, writer, assignment manager and documentary producer. She has been the recipient of several Emmys, Associated Press and Press Club awards for newscasts and news documentaries in television and radio. She played a major role in WCAU TV-CBS coverage of the city of Philadelphia's bombing of the MOVE compound in 1985, for which the station won the national prestigious Alfred I. DuPont Award.

She was recipient of a national Telly Award for a Food Network documentary, Daring Dining, for the show *The Best Of*, for which she was a researcher, writer and producer. Her documentary work also has appeared on the History and Fine Living channels.

She is a regular contributor to *Cape May Magazine* as a feature writer, has written for Montgomery County (Pennsylvania) *Town & Country Magazine* and is a member of the Garden Writers of America.

Karen lives in Cape May and Blue Bell, Pennsylvania, with her husband, landscape architect John E. Schneider, and two Labrador retrievers, Cubby and Coco.

Bibliography

BOOKS/BOOKLETS
Cape May Queen of the Seaside Resorts, Its History and Architecture by George E. Thomas and Carl Doebley
His Hour Upon the Stage – the Story of the Civil War Horse Soldier and the Woman Who Fought to Save his Life by Mary Hennessy
General A. P. Hill, the Story of a Confederate Soldier by James I. Robertson Jr
The Cape May Handbook by Carolyn Pitts, Michael Fish, Hugh J. McCauley and Trina Vaux
The Chalfonte by Helena LeFroy Caperton
Black Hawk Down by Mark Bowden

PERIODICALS
Austin Daily Statesman
Baltimore Sun
Cape May Magazine
Cape May Star and Wave
Cape May Wave
Cape May County Herald
McClure's
National Geographic
Philadelphia Inquirer
Philadelphia Magazine
Richmond News Leader
Richmond Times Dispatch
Roanoke Times
The Magazine of Albermarle History
Press of Atlantic City
Newsweek
Time
Town and Country

LIBRARIES & ARCHIVES
Encyclopedia Virginia – Appomattox Campaign
Hollins University Archives
Monticello Library
National Archives
National Register of Historic Places in Virginia
National Park Service
Social Register of Virginia
University of Maryland School of Architecture, Planning and Preservation Archives
University of Pennsylvania Library
Virginia Military Institute

WEBSITES
capemay.com
chalfonte.com
civilwarphotos.net
civil-war.net
ushistory.org
virginia.edu